MY TAKE

1

Rafael E. Evangelista

May 2023

....

Author

About the author:
Rafael E. Evangelista is a retired capital partner of Baker McKenzie, the largest international law firm in the world.

This is the resume' of Rafael E. Evangelista –

Lawyer, banker, diplomat.
Co-founder, Task Force Good Governance;

Board member, Bank of Commerce (former vice-chairman and executive committee member);

Various memberships in corporate boards including the Rizal Chapter and the Makati branch of the Philippine National Red Cross;

Board chairman of the NOVA Foundation for the Less Abled;

National Commander, Defenders of Bataan and

Corregidor;

and Honorary Consul of the Republic of Lithuania
to the the Philippines.

Retired Capital Partner, Baker & Mckenzie
(international law practice),
and Member, Board of Trustees, Ateneo de
Manila
University.

Attended Ateneo de Manila University (A.B.,
LI.B.),
Georgetown University (Master of Laws), with an
honorary Ph.D. from St. Louis University.
Recipient
of the Lithuanian Congressional Gold Medal of
Honor.

....

Dedication

Dedication I would like to dedicate this first, and
hopefully not last, compendium of essays and poetry
written by me to the following:

1. My parents, **Dr. Rafael E Evangelista** and
Encarnacion E. Evangelista. My father was a real life
war hero and a medical doctor who healed at no cost to
his patients. In many ways, he was my life's inspiration
of "service to others." My mom was the first real writer in
the family. It was she who first encouraged me to write at
an early age.

2) My sister, **Rhona E. Centeno**, the other real
writer in the family with my mom. She won multiple
award for her literary writings. She graduated with two
Summa Cum Laude degrees, both completed in four
years.

3) **Father Joseph O'Hare S.J.** was my freshman professor in English. He was a pillar of encouragement to my writing. He was the first person who insisted that I publish my works.

4) **Father Miguel Bernad S.J.** was the moderator of the Heights, the literary publication of the Ateneo. He caused the publication of some of my works to encourage me to share my writings with others.

I dedicate this book to these five persons who played such a singular role, each of them, in my literary life. Thank you.

....

Preface and Acknowledgment

Writing has been a passion of mine for almost as long as I can remember. I recall writing essays, short stories and poems as early as the age of 12 years.

Unfortunately, collecting and publishing whatever I had written never warranted the same attention I had given to writing them. Many, if not most of my articles and poems were lost over the years, with little recollection on my part of what, when, and where I wrote. Only a few were ever published.

Most of what I wrote had been scribbled on notebooks and left to fade on forgotten bookshelves. With the advent of computers and cellular phones, my writings were confined to the memory banks of these machines. As the machines turned obsolete, whatever writings were in them were simply confined to oblivion because I never transcribed what I had written.

Obviously, printing and publishing what I had written in the past did not occupy any position of priority in my mind's scheme of things.

I had been writing for many, many years simply for the joy of writing, and the joy of writing was for my self-fulfillment alone. I felt no need to share my thoughts, my dreams, my ambitions with anyone.

Or so I thought!

An old Jesuit professor of mine, Fr. Joseph O'Hare, S.J., who went on to become the President of Fordham University years later, was the first person to jiggle the notion that writing is only half the task of, well, writing! He told my parents at the end of my freshman year at the Ateneo de Manila University that their son was "intellectually selfish." He told them that I had refused to publish anything I had written, even in the school literary digests. The term he actually used to describe me was "intellectual bum."

Fr O'Hare complained to my parents that I had shown no interest in publishing, and hence in sharing, any of my writings. In so many words, he was telling my parents that while I had the talent to write, I was too selfish to share. Fr O'Hare's words did not sink in for many years.

A few years afterwards, another Jesuit professor, Fr. Miguel Bernad S.J., actually had some of my pieces published in the literary magazine of the Ateneo, The Heights, without my knowledge. As before, I had no interest in publishing what I wrote. And Fr. Bernad felt he had to take matters into his own hands.

Giving back was all this fuss was about. My two Jesuit professors and my parents were complicit in reminding me through the years that if someone had been given a gift, the gift was meant to be shared. Writing was only half of my life's mission of writing. Publishing and sharing with others completed the giving back required.

Although I have self published a number of Haiku poetry books over the past couple of years, this book "My Take 1" is the first comprehensive presentation of my writings - essays and poetry alike. For this effort, I have a new found friend, Jobo Elizes, from across the seas in the United States who encouraged me to publish this book, and beyond that, offered to publish the book himself.

I am grateful to my parents, Fathers O'Hare and Miguel Bernad S.J., and Jobo Elizes for all their encouragement that finally resulted in the publication of this book. I am likewise very grateful to have been afforded the opportunity of giving back and sharing with others, and hope my efforts are worth the reader's while. Rafael E Evangelista 12 May 2023

Contents

....

1
My Song Is For You, Lord

I dedicate this poem to all those who have lived a full God filled life:

My Song Is For You, Lord

*I have the words.
When will the music come?
I want to sing my song
Before the setting sun.*

2

Come strum the music, Lord,
So I can put my words to song
Of praise, and love, and joy;
I have waited for so long.

Oh Lord, I hear distant strains,
A beautiful melody I hear.
It is the music of the wind
Whispering gently in my ear.

Help me sing my song, O Lord,
The words I have within me.
By Your grace, the wind is singing
My song that's meant to be.

Words I started writing
Since I was a little boy,
Oh Lord, hear my song
Of praise, of love and joy.

Now as the sun begins to fade,
And I am growing old,
And the wind begins its song,
My story will be told.

You have strummed the music.
Please put my words to song.
The song, my Lord, is for You.
I have waited for so long.

(Rafael E Evangelista, 18 July 2020)

....

I Love You Now And Always Will

I Love You Now And Always Will
Though it did take some time
For you to feel love's sunshine,
I'm glad it did not take forever
To share your heart with mine.
Open your arms, and embrace

The truth that I love you so.
Open your eyes and see
The world around us glow.
Come with me and hold me
Close to you today, tomorrow.
God meant us to be always one,

Through any joy or sorrow.
Open your arms, enfold me
In your tightest embrace.
Be mine forever, joined
In love's warming grace.
I love you and i always will

Through all my remaining years.
Please know I will love you still
Through laughter and tears.
I am growing on in years,
But growing old is not a fear,
As long as you are at my side,
As long as you are near.

At 82, I love you still.
Beyond 82, I always will!

(REE, 26 Feb 2023)

....

3
THE MORAL RESPONSE OF THE PEOPLE

A barangay is many things, but it is not an island. It must not be. A barangay is the basic building block of the riches and of the forces and the ferment that shape the nation and its people. A barangay is the transmission of what is best and must be preserved. A barangay is an instrument for the growth and the transformation of a county that is rapidly in process. A barangay is situated itself at the crossroads of action within the nation and shares in the nation's excitements and frustrations, in the nation's glory and despair, and is shaped as well by the nation's triumphs as by its agonies. A barangay is a bridge that links the country with the movement and growth around the nation. A barangay, in other words, is the Filipino and the Philippines. Therefore a barangay's concerns and priorities are dictated and shaped by the concerns of the people and nation it serves. It is this privileged role and privileged position that is the wellspring of the excitement that can, and should, grip a barangay.

Today, what is it that is agitating people and nation? Although it is the popular thing to do these days, I shall not speak of an inhospitable government. Neither am I prepared to endorse the almost idyllic description of a garden paradise made in a recent election victory speeches. Nor need I repeat what has been said more than once about the economy or what parliamentarians of the street are shouting about political life.

Only the intentionally myopic can fail to detect the economic and political ills that plague the land. All these demand attention. They demand analysis. They demand reflection. They clamor for solution. It is in this context that we suggest that a barangay must respond within the limits of its capacity. In truth, the barangay is meant to be our first responder to the myriad of concerns that our nation is faced with. But, what kind of response?

Without doubt an intellectual and technical response. Beyond the technical and intellectual, however, the barangay is asked to give more. The barangay is asked to bring to bear upon the problems of the nation every moral resource at its command. The moral response, to my mind, s the more pressing task. It is my conviction that, while the economic and political problems that beset us are of enormous magnitude, they are at root symptoms of a more deep-seated disease. The disease, if not vigorously attended to, can be fatal to our life as a nation. As has been so aptly put:

We are facing "the erosion of the anthropological foundations which ground the possibility of civil society." What we are facing is "a situation where the indispensable bases for an authentically democratic and Christian society are radically being undermined.

What are the anthropological foundations of civil society? Basically they are four: truth, justice, peace, love. These foundations have been violently shaken. Thus, 1) In the conduct of public affairs truth has been badly battered. People have learned to believe as true the exact opposite of what is officially announced. And when the untruth is made public it is hypocritically given the semblance of an honorable disguise. 2) Justice has been brutalized beyond recognition. The lady of justice has been stripped of her blindfold and the balance scales are often replaced by the truncheon or by the barrel of a gun. 3)The meaning of peace has been distorted. Peace has come to mean the desolation of a hamletted village or the grim visage of a silenced salvage victim. 4) Love at best has come to manifest itself in the shape of wasteful display and at worst in human sacrifice at the altar of national security.

And it is in this critical context that we, the people, are challenged to make a contribution. We have been, by God's grace, provided with a vehicle to achieve and reinstall the four foundations of civil society in our country – the barangay. Today, let us ask ourselves. What is it that we as Filipinos can offer to our communities and our country through the barangay? (REE, 2 July 2020)

....

4
TESTIMONIAL FOR FILIPINO WORLD WAR II VETERANS

Most Filipinos are unaware that there is a number of their countrymen, war veterans all, who are recipients of one of the two highest awards granted by the US Government. These awardees are Filipino veterans of WW II, who have been awarded the United States Congressional Gold Medal, the highest civilian award given by the United States.

My father, Dr Rafael L Evangelista, is one of those veterans who have been so honored.

The US Congressional Gold Medal should be distinguished from the US Medal of Honor, which is the highest military award granted by the US Congress.

But both are in the same level of category and honor, and both are the highest awards granted by the United States. Both are worthy of equal esteem and respect.

It should be noted that Filipino awardees of the US Congressional Gold Medal are in the exulted company of George Washington, the first ever awardee of this Gold Medal.

What the Congressional Gold Medal really means (from the official citation):

Citation:
Description The Congressional Gold Medal is an award bestowed by the United States Congress. It is Congress's highest expression of national appreciation for distinguished achievements and contributions by individuals or institutions.

Presented by: United States Congress CATEGORY OF: THE CONRESSIONAL MEDAL OF HONOR

1. It is of the same category as the highest US military honor: the Congressional Medal of Honor;
2. It is bestowed by the United States Congress;
3. It is the United States Congress' highest expression of national appreciation for distinguished achievements and contributions.

I share this citation with you so that we can truly appreciate the sacrifices that our war veterans, like my father, made during WW II in the Philippines.
Raf Evangelista Former National Commander, Defenders of Bataan & Corregidor 25 March 2023

....

5

Sinagtala

The spread of authoritarianism starts when people are silenced. Free speech is the first freedom citizens lose.
The best way we know to combat this is to continue to fight for the Truth and the right to spread it.
And democracy needs your help. Historical revisionism and the distortion, and even the denial, of the truth is on going even now. It will only accelerate,

Unless We Make A Stand! Let us all make a stand for the truth NOW!

Death of the sinagtala, Death of the fireflies in the skies Death of the rainbows Death of the wind's gentle sighs.

What happened to us once before When wrong people came to power, Can happen again if we fail to fight! Our children, their families will suffer!

Some feign ignorance and disaffection. How can they sit back and not dare? Our heroes died in the field of sacrifice. Beyond fearful, some just don't care!

On our land, the sun will either rise or set. What is it that we wish to preside over? If we do not now have the backbone, Our country could be lost forever.

The sun disappeared from sight before. Shall we let darkness set on us again? But that is what our country is facing Unless we make a stand now, not then.

We dream of stars shining in our skies, Of the sun again lighting up our day. Let us stand strong together as one And let God's bidding guide our way.

"Para sa Diyos at Bayan," our cry, In glorious battle and blessed peace. Bring back the sinagtala and rainbows. Love for country should never cease. (Raffy Evangelista, 28 November 2021)

....

6
A Reminder About Democracy

The 1986 People's Revolution was not so much about individuals gaining or losing power, or about colors whether yellow, blue, green or whatever. It was more about the people fighting to reclaim their democratic rights. That fight is not over. That fight must go on for so long as there are politicians who arrogate unto themselves the power to rule.

The survival of true Democracy- governance of, for and by the citizenry – depends on how we defend and implement the Constitution. The Constitution, empowers the people to govern, seeking to do away with the erroneous decades old conclusion that proper democratic governance is one of leadership, that the sole democratic prerogative of citizens is the right to vote.

True Democracy means the Governance of, for, and by the Citizenry. It does not mean the Governance of Leadership. But no Constitution is self-executing. No law is. The power of the fundamental law rests in the people's collective readiness to wield it as a shield – as though their lives depended on it – not just when freedom and the rule of law are threatened, but in the political fiber of their everyday lives. Today, and everyday, is a good day to remind ourselves of our collective role and duty in our Democracy.

The elected and appointed leaders in a true Democracy are servants of the people. They are not rulers. They have the obligation to follow and implement the wishes of the people, the real bosses in a Democracy. They cannot dictate and implement their own programs of government against the wishes of the citizens. To allow otherwise is feudalism at best, not democracy. This in turn often leads to populism which as history bears witness to, can end in Dictatorships. Leaders who do not acknowledge that they are servants, not rulers, are a threat to our democratic way of life.

The current indifference of the citizenry and the non-acquiescence of leaders to their role as servants of the people can lead to the demise of Democracy. Citizens will become steadily disenchanted with their democratic systems. As a result, they will be more and more willing to vote for extremist politicians who promise to break with the status quo. A vicious political cycle ensues.

Today, satisfaction with Democracy, according to the report, has eroded in most parts of the world, with an especially notable drop over the past decade. Public confidence in Democracy is at the lowest point on record in the United States, the major Democracies of Western Europe, sub-Saharan Africa, and Latin America. In some countries, including the United States, this metric is now reaching an important threshold: The number of people who are dissatisfied with Democracy is greater than the number of people who are satisfied with it.

In the Philippines, that metric may even be more dismal. Most people have come to believe that they have no required role to play in the country's democracy. Even voting, including voting for true servant leaders, seems to have lost importance in our processes of governance.

It is perfectly possible that Democracies will recover from their current crisis in the years to come. But every new data point makes it that much harder to deny that such a crisis exists. Without the people's participation in its defense, we very well could see the demise of Republican Democracy. We must not stand idly by and let that happen! (Raf Evangelista, 25 February 2020)

....

7
The First And Last Times

Two things I will never forget:
The way you looked
At me the first time,
And the way you looked
At me the last time.

I always watched…
I always watched
And then only acted.
I always watched

*With a still heart
And mind…
And I thought
I had learned.*

*When I thought I had
Watched enough,
And learned enough,
I felt I could act upon
The knowledge
I had gained.
But sadly,
It turns out that
I could not.*

*When I reached out
To touch you,
You were gone.
I did not act upon
The knowledge gained.
I saw you for a moment.
I saw the way you looked
At me the first time.
But then I missed the
Way you looked at me
The last time.*

*Then you were gone!
Sadly, I looked away
The time you looked
At me for the last time.
And when I looked back
You were gone
For the very Last time.*

*The last time that
Broke my heart!*

(Raffy Evangelista, 29 April 2023)

....

8
Colors

Quite frankly, I do not agree that people should be typed by the color of their skin. To begin with, there is no such thing as a "White" person. Put a white sheet of paper beside any "White" man. He will most certainly not be white. The so called "White" man is pink and all the shades from there to flushed red. So when some, and there are many, talk about people of color" to refer to the brown, black and yellow populations, the little bell of racism in my brain starts ringing.

Wittingly or unwittingly, the phrases "I am White" and you are a "Person of Color" is racism itself at its most insidious. It translates to "I am White! I am special and unique! All other races are colored and belong to the "crass hoipoloi." The expression of "People of Color" has become to some "White" people a pejorative to discriminate against non-whites. But these "White" bigots fail to realize and understand that they too are people of color. They too are non-whites!

Sadly, not being black has fairly recently become an issue for some African Americans who resent that they have been relegated to the tail end of the race color spectrum, and therefore resent all non blacks. As a consequence African Americans are venting their resentment against Asian Americans, who the the blacks feel are the "johnny come latelies in the migratory spectrum."

Will the roll of the dice end here? It is very probable that Asian Americans will themselves start pushing back when they have no where to go. Americans do not realize that Asian Americans, including Fil Ams, were among the first people to migrate to America, long before the white Pilgrims did. So much for staking a color claim.

And at the end of it all, I am left wondering what the color of God is! (Raffy Evangelista, 28 April 2023)

....

9
Haiku: Nightfall Meditation

As the shadows fall,
Clouds drift about the
mountain sides,
Searching for the moon.

Crimson and gold hues
Streak the dark purple heavens,
Beckoning the stars.

Sea waves lap unseen
In the setting dusk of night,
Singing their haunting song.

A solitary
Bird calls out to the moon
To bid it good night.

The echo of night
Sings out to the evening sky,
As stars blink goodnight.

I call to my God
That the sun will raise once more
His Golden Scepter!

(Raf Evangelista, 25 February 202

....

10
Lux In Domino
(Light In The Lord)

Each one of us is a star.
Even if sometimes, nights
Take our shine away;
Even if clouds and rain
Try to drown our light.

Sometimes we shine
With the rest; and
Sometimes we twinkle alone.
Shine and realize
That we may be the only
Light for someone
In times of darkness.

Be the light that
Can only see good...
Be the light that forgives
The worst...
Be the light that forgets
The bad...
Be the light that fights
Evil...
Be the light in the Lord!

As our country journeys
in these uncertain
times groping its way,
Be the light of our faith.
Let our light of love
Give others the hope
To see life through.

Lux in Domino,
The Light that shines
On and for others.
Let our light be the
Light of the Lord!

(REE, 19 September 2020)

....

11
Real Love

I dedicate this love poem I wrote to all my relatives and friends as a reminder to love one another as God loves us.-

*His Love turned darkness
Into brightness of pure Light.
His Splendor banished sadness
And the loneliness of night.
The perfect Love Day is not
What man declares it to be.*

*True Love occurred before that
When He was nailed to the tree.
Blood flowed from His Heart above,
As He hang dying on that tree,
He bought our lives with His love
Removing sin from you and me.*

*Perfect love He gave when He died.
Revealing to us how He truly cared.
Can we spread love, can we even try,
The way He gave, the way He shared?
Sharing love is all He asks we give.
"Give love as I give you life," He said;*

"My love I shared you did receive.

Give to others before the sun is fled."
The real Love Day is when
He gave His Love to free both you and me,
And sacrificed His Life to save us
All that distant day on Calvary.

(REE, 14 February 2021)

....

12
Tongue in Cheek

A legislator in the Philippines is either a Senatong or representa-thief.

The Philippines is known for the giant crocodile, called buwaya locally. Senatongs and Representathieves are also called buwayas. This is because they have huge appetites, and are so ravenous and insatiable.

There are also many pigs in the country. Pork is one of the major food industries of the country. In fact, the buwayas love and protect their pork. So much so that the poor in the Philippines continue to get poorer and the starving continue to get hungrier. That is because buwayas keep all the pork to themselves.

They consume so much pork that the buwayas are starting to look like pigs. Hence, a new name is taking hold: Babuwayas, to describe them. And that is why Congress in the Philippines is called a Pigsty or Babuyan! (REE, 18 Sept 2013)

....

13
SONG TO MY FATHER

I have the words within me.

Is the music ready to play?
I must sing your song before
My own evening turns to gray.
The wind strums the music,
Now I can put my words to song

To proclaim how much I love you.
I have waited for so long.
Dad, those distant strains
Of beautiful melodies I hear.
It is your music in the wind,
Still whispering in my ear.

Let me sing this song for you,
The words I have within me.
The song that the wind is singing,
Is your song that was meant to be.
Integrity, courage and love…
These are words I still recall,

Lessons that you taught me
When I was just so very small.
You taught me to be humble,
You taught me to be strong …
And that both go together, even
If sometimes things go wrong.

Giving was your gift to others,
And service to all in need…
It was lessons you imparted
By thought, word and deed.
I feel you present in my heart,
I am what I am because of you.

And even if you have departed,
Your lessons still ring true.
Your life has long since faded
As your world slowly grew old.
The wind is singing your song,

Now your story should be told.

The story shall continue
Even now that you are gone.
Your song will long continue
After the setting of the sun.
The wind sings so gently of
My source of strength and love.

The song, Father, is about you.
Please bless me from above.
Love you, Dad!

(Rafael E Evangelista, 21 October 2020)

....

14
Racism Against Asian Americans, Including FilAms

The growing incidence of racism against Asian Americans is so distressing. But racism against Asians, specially Filipinos, is not a recent happening.

American racism against Filipinos dates back for over 120 years.

Remember when Filipinos were displayed in G strings at the New Orleans World Fair? Then there was the massacre of Filipino migrant workers in California (for dating white women), the reference to Filipinos as "monkeys" without tails; and the blanket claim by some white Americans that Filipinos who fought in WW II were all cowards. And what was the pretext given to justify US colonization of the Philippines? "To christianize and educate the savages in those islands." Ironically, these "savages" were largely Christianized and cultured by then. The list of racism incidents against Filipinos goes on and on.

To this day. Most Americans do not know or understand that, unlike other Asian countries, the Philippines was forcibly colonized in 1898 by the US. During that period, until 1946 when independence was finally granted, Filipinos were American nationals and, for those who travelled abroad, holders of US passports. No other Asian group fall into this category. The Philippines was the first, and officially the only colony of the United States. Filipinos are the only Asians who at one time in their history were American nationals.

Despite being forcibly colonized by the US, despite the fact that Filipinos fought the Philippine American War against American invaders only a few decades before WW II, and despite the fact that thousands of Filipinos lost their lives in their fight for freedom against the American colonizers, the Philippines threw in their lot to fight with and for America in WW II. The Philippines lost over a million of its young fighters and Filipinos civilians in WW II. Filipinos fought and/or sacrificed their lives, not only for the Philippines, but also for the US.

America still has to understand that the decision of the Philippines/US to stand together during WW II was less a decision of the United States to save the Philippines in the cause of Freedom and Democracy, as it was a decision of the Philippines to fight with the US. After all, Japan had promised the Philippines "independence," (which the Filipinos had long been fighting for) within the "Japanese Co-Prosperity Sphere" proposed by the Japanese. Filipinos could have easily sided with Japan in WW II against their "American oppressors" and gone with Japan who promised them immediate "freedom." If the Philippines had done so, there is arguably the possibility that America would have lost WW II. But that is another story.

In a limited sense, some recognition has been given by America to Filipino Veterans who fought in WW II. They were awarded in 2017 the highest civilian award that US Congress can give - the US Congressional Gold

Medal, the first ever recipient of which was President George Washington himself. They were given that medal not just as Filipinos, but as American nationals as well. Incomplete recognition at best, but this USCGM in a way confirms a right of FilAms to reside in the US. They are after all, in a manner of speaking, "Gold Medal" FilAm descendants of their Filipino/American Veteran forebearers.

FilAms can point to the "trial by combat" that their Veteran forebearers went through in WW II. They can assert that their forebearers fought in that War not simply as Filipinos but as American nationals, not simply for the Philippines, but for America. As an Asian American veteran (not a FilAm) declared as he showed his scars of war on TV: "Is this patriot(ic) enough?"

I hasten to point out another fact. Thousands of Filipinos are even now in the forefront of another war for the US. Thousands of Filipino nurses and doctors are quietly fighting the Pandemic War today as medical frontliners. In California alone, there are at last count over 30,000 nurses on the Pandemic frontlines. If all FilAm medical frontliners in the US came home to the Philippines today because of the threat of racism, the health systems of some States of the Union, and maybe the US itself, could collapse and many more Americans would perish.

Historically too, Filipino settlements existed in the America long before the Pilgrims came. The arrival of the Pilgrims is, of course, the corner stone of White America's claim to the US. But the ties between Filipinos and America started long before the Pilgrims arrived. If Filipinos arrived in America before the Pilgrims, America has no basis for demanding that FilAms return to where they came from.

It is interesting but few people know that there may be linguistic and cultural ties between Filipinos and Native Americans. Take the similarities between Tagalog/other Philippine dialects and certain Native American languages. In the North Dakota Sioux language, the word for mother is "Ina", as it is in Tagalog. Do these language similarities give credence to the claim that migrations from our part of the world are, by virtue of sea and overland travel, related to Native Americans? Maybe so. Maybe our ancestors landed in America long, long before the Pilgrims did. Maybe they were there when Native Americans came to be.

I would like to add one other personal observation on "Race."

Quite frankly, I do not agree that people should be typed by the color of their skin. To begin with, there is no such thing as a "White" person. Put a white sheet of paper beside any "White" man. He will most certainly not be white. The so called "White" man is pink and all the shades from there to flushed red. So when some, and there are many, talk about people of color" to refer to the brown, black and yellow populations, the little bell of racism in my brain starts ringing.

Wittingly or unwittingly, the phrases "I am White" and you are a "Person of Color" is racism itself at its most insidious. It translates to "I am White! I am special and unique! All other races are colored and belong to the "hoipoloi." "People of Color" has become to some "White" people a pejorative to discriminate against non-whites. But these "White" bigots fail to realize and understand that they too are people of color. They too are non-whites!

Looking at legislation passed in the early years of America, it is clear that racism through legislation was a basic tenet that States like Virginia and Maryland implemented to create a privileged class of citizens that came to be what is now known as the "White Race." This legislation not only condoned and permitted slavery of "Black and Colored People", but enshrined the so called superiority of the "White Race." Under threat of severe penalties, people from the "Colored Races" could not marry or have sex with the "Whites." "Colored" persons could not vote run for public office or own property. As late as 1937, even Native Americans were not allowed to vote ... on the ground that they were not citizens!

In the 1950's, "Colored" people had to give up their seats to "White" people on crowded buses. Only "Whites" could sit in the front sections of those buses. I share an anecdote about a grandfather of mine, Col. Jose N Evangelista. Col Evangelista was the first Filipino Commandant and Superintendent of the Philippine Constabulary Academy (later the Philippine Military Academy) years before WW II and before Rosa Banks.This was during the period when the Philippines was still a colony of the US.

Col Evangelista was sent on a military mission to the US. He was riding public transportation in the full uniform of an officer in the US Army in Washington DC when he was told to move to the rear of the bus. His response was: "If I am entitled to use this uniform, I am entitled to sit in the front of this bus," and stayed where he was. But my grandfather was a rare exception. Few "Colored" persons were granted Officer rank in the US Army during his time.

It is unfortunate that today many "People of Color" have swallowed the lie, hook, line and sinker, that race is a determining factor of one's status in American society. It isn't, and certainly shouldn't be. Love, not race, is the determining factor in any family, in any community, and in any society. And love has no color.

In a spillover of the "war of colors," it is unfortunate that the war has taken a grotesque turn for the worse. Where the war before was principally between the "white" race and "people of color," the trend of late has been racist attacks by the "blacks" against Asian Americans or the yellow and brown races. The so called "people of color" are turning against one another.

Racism must stop in the United States. Because if it continues, "United" will be "Divided." And a "Divided States" will not survive!

The story of the relations between the US and the Philippines is a long, and sometimes a rocky, one. There is so much more to that story that can be written about here. But that story is one that most Fil Ams should learn about if they wish to claim their rightful place in American Society!

(Raffy Evangelista, 12 April 2021) (Rafael E Evangelista is a retired Capital Partner of the International Law Firm of Baker & McKenzie, An immediate past National Commander of the Defenders of Bataan & Corregidor)

....

15
My Inner Core

I have collected moments
Of time and of love,
Seeds planted by gentle winds
Sent from high above.
The seeds have grown towering
Beyond the clouds drifting,
Floating, dancing, or so it seems,
In and out of my shifting dreams.

The morning light softly shines
Through mists of my awakening.
The gold of the morning sun
Slides into my mind singing
To the day that has just begun.
I wonder what the day has in store.
Shall I ask for less, or maybe more,
As birds sing and night is done?

I have faced inner withering
With recharged vitality of life.
I shall never surrender my being
To crossfires of stress and strife.
I feel the warmth in my inner core
Of the distant mountains touching

The sun rising from distant shores.
The night clouds retreat gathering
Last memories of dark receding
From my being …

My inner core.

Raf Evangelista 22 March 2023

....

16
Spread the Truth

I wrote this piece sometime ago. Portions of it may still be relevant to the times today: Spread The Truth!

The spread of authoritarianism starts when people are silenced. Free speech is the first freedom citizens lose. And Truth is trampled upon. That is what happened when Martial Rule was proclaimed by Ferdinand E Marcos.

The best way we know to combat a repetition of this tragic episode in our country, where thousands were killed or imprisoned and the Country's coffers drained dry, is to continue to fight for the Truth and the right to spread it.

Will history repeat itself? Will Junior follow his Senior? Only if we let the Son muddy up the pages of history. Only if we do not fight revisionism and and the distortion of the truth. Only if we let him and do nothing. But the Son could try to set up his own populist regime. It is possible he will, though not necessarily through the mechanism of Martial Law.

And Democracy needs our help. Democracy and Freedom will die without the Truth. Historical revisionism and the distortion, and even the denial, of the Truth is on going even now. It accelerated as we moved toward, through, and beyond the National Elections. It is accelerating even now. Let us all make a stand. Let us decide, despite the results of the elections, to continue to stand up for Truth and Democracy!

If Junior has similar ambitions as Senior, he need not even declare Martial Law like his Dad. All he needs is Federalism and Political Dynasties.

Charter change to Federalism and while continuing to espouse Political Dynasties could be a perfect recipie for national disaster. A dire forecast is that the government of each federal state could be controlled by political dynasties. With the National Government, and federal state governments, rotationally dominated by political dynasties, continuing control from the top of the power pyramid of government by select family groups can be assured.

Even now, after the last national elections, and even without Federalism in place, more and more political dynasties have been elected into power, most with connections to BBM and Digong. Federalism, with autonomous or semi autonomous states, sitting below the national government, can only exacerbate the situation of centralized control. Specially where the national government and the governments of each state form a cabal to consolidate and perpetuate themselves in power. It is not farfetched to autocratic or populist groups could, and would, utilize this lethal combination to perpetuate themselves in power.

If it happens, so much for the constitutional mandate that Sovereignty resides in the people, and all governmental authority emanates from them. This mandate will be trashed in all but words by those who would want to stay in control forever.

Watch out too for the repeal or radical amendment of the Local Government Code which gives flesh to the constitutional dictate that sovereignty resides in the people. The LGC proclaims the barangay as the basic unit of government. Contrary to what is happening even today, nothing can, or should, happen in any barangay without the approval of the Barangay

Assembly. The Assembly is the highest body in a Barangay, not the Barangay Chairman or his Barangay Council. It is noteworthy that the Barangay Assembly is comprised in membership by all residents of the barangay. Technically, the Assembly should not be under the dictates of city, provincial or national government above. This is Democracy at work, with the power flowing from bottom up.

Let us guard against the now revived move to create a federal government. And continue to fight to de-insitutionalize political dynasties once and for all! (Raf Evangelista, 20 May 2022) ∘

....

17
Reminising Law practice in the 60s

Just found this in my files. Am sending it to you in case you may be interested in using it (or excerpts thereof) in the book - Rafael "Raf" Erum Evangelista

Raf Evangelista was one of the pioneers of the law profession in cross country law in the Philippines at a time when few professionals in that country ever conceived of advising on this branch of law.

Try to imagine the early to mid sixties - a world without Internet and fast communications. In many ways, the first wave of non-U.S. born lawyers who joined Russell Baker's burgeoning law firm in the early sixties and started advising U.S.-based clients on cross-border issues could be likened to pilots crossing the Atlantic solo without instruments. Databases -including statutory legal materials- were in their infancy. Any information had to be gathered essentially manually from sources far and between. Telephone conference calls covering multiple jurisdictions were largely non-existent. Yet, the greater challenge to overcome by far was the credibility factor.

Again please v sualize a bunch of young lawyers , each from a different country and culture and a strange accent uprooted and replanted in small offices in various cities across the US. Their original roots included countries such as Germany, Italy, Spain, England, Mexico and Canada to name only a few, but also more far-flung jurisdictions such as India, Taiwan, Brazil and The Philippines.

Surely, these pioneers had many detractors. In the eyes of the local bar and establishment, both in the United States and elsewhere, they must have appeared overly bold and audacious. How could any of these unconventional, often raw characters have the audacity to advise on U.S. soil regarding legal matters which only lawyers located in the foreign jurisdiction could legitimately handle.

Yet, the vision of Russell Baker was that an individual born or raised abroad , once trained in the laws and judicial system of his native jurisdiction, when relocating to the United States and obtaining a law degree, could offer to U.S. clients and colleagues, both inside and outside the Firm, a new approach, one that involved a comparative analysis and practical advice unavailable elsewhere in the legal community of the times.

Raf Evangelista was one of these early pioneers. He was born in 1940 in the Philippines. He attended the Ateneo de Manila University where he obtained his Bachelor of Laws, and Georgetown University where he finished with a Masters of Laws. He was also awarded a Doctorate of Laws from St. Louis University in the late seventies. Raf has lectured at American University and the George Washington University in Washington, DC, and at the Ateneo de Manila University in the Philippines.

Russell Baker, who was in search of non-US legal talent, learned of Raf's presence in the mid sixties at Georgetown Law School via Washington DC partners, Walter Slowiniski and Mike Waris. While at Georgetown U, Raf became an associate of the Firm's D.C. after he was invited by Walter and Mike, both professors at GU to join the DC Office.

As the story goes, when Raf returned to the Philippines, Russell deputized Manila partner, Luis Guerrero, to assure that Raf would join the Manila Office with the words "Get Raf" 1966. It is reported that the brief meeting between Louie and Raf took place in the Manila Office of the Firm, and that, with little discussion, Raf agreed to join that office.

So after his stint with the Washington D.C office, Raf started officially with the Manila Office in 1966. During his tenure with the Manila Office, the Manila Office grew from a small law office of 6 or 7 lawyers to a middle/large sized law firm, and joined the mainstream of Baker & McKenzie's practice of "cross country" law.

One of the conditions for his joining the Manila Office was that he would be admitted to the a US State Bar. Subsequent to his joining the Manila Office, Raf was admitted to the New York State Bar.

Raf also spent a total of two years as a Partner of the HongKong Office of Baker & McKenzie from 1972 to 1974.

Baker McKenzie, the largest international law firm in the world, is today comprised by lawyers like Rafael E. Evangelista.

The following is a resume of Rafael E. Evangelista

- Lawyer, banker, diplomat. Co-founder, Task Force Good Governance;

Board member, Bank of Commerce (former vice-chairman and executive committee member);

Various memberships in corporate boards including the Rizal Chapter and the Makati branch of the Philippine National Red Cross;

Board chairman of the NOVA Foundation for the Less Abled;

National Commander, Defenders of Bataan and Corregidor;

and Honorary Consul of the Republic of Lithuania to the the Philippines.

Retired Capital Partner, Baker & Mckenzie (international law practice),

and Member, Board of Trustees, Ateneo de Manila University.

Attended Ateneo de Manila University (A.B., Ll.B.), Georgetown University (Master of Laws), with an honorary Ph.D. from St. Louis University.

Recipient of the Lithuanian Congressional Gold Medal of Honor.

....

18
In the corner of your heart

In The Corner Of Your Heart
And when I pass, look for me,
Even if we are physically apart.
Look to where I shall always be,
A smile in the corner of your heart.

(REE, March 15, 2021)

....

19
Broken Crayons (poem)

*A throbbing heart is a fragile heart
That can be filled with bitterness
Or joy. The choice is often yours.
You can chose to mend and start,
And fill your lives with loveliness
By painting a different course.*

*There are hiccups along the way –
Pain, anger, and stumbling blocks.
Paint only smiles of the early sun.
Hold on to its bright golden rays,
And banish those painful shocks
Along blighted paths you've run.*

*Broken crayons can paint the sky
In colors - red, blue and green,
There is much that a heart can do:
Forget hurt, paint sunshine, or try.
Light in shade that flits unseen,
Can be painted as rainbows too.*

*Colors change the world we live in.
Let us look beyond the bend.
Let us paint roses and clover,
Not shadows of what has been.
Keep painting. Darkness will end,
If you spread the light all over.*

*Hold hands, and never let go.
Your broken crayons and mine
Can still paint rainbows just like so,
And make this world of ours shine…
Paint, dear friend, paint! Go on!
Paint the sun with broken crayons!*

Raffy Evangelista 12 June 2022

……………………………………..

20
Testimonial For Dr Rafael L. Evangelista, My Father, A War Hero

I am posting an update of an article I wrote a few years ago about my father and his role in WW II. I simply wanted the younger generations of Evangelistas to know that the family had an ascendant who heroically served in WW II. -

Dr. Rafael L Evangelista And The 31st Infantry Division, A Story of Heroism, World War II -

My father, Capt. Rafael L Evangelista (Lolo Apeng to our family) was with the 31st Infantry Division that played a key role in the defense of the Abucay, Bataan. He was with the Medical Corps of the USAFFE. After Abucay, he was assigned to the General Field Hospital (No 1?) in Mariveles, Bataan.

My father always had a fascination with native herbal medicine and edible plants. This served him in good stead in the latter part of the defense of Bataan. The Allies, by that time, were running short of both food and medicine. My father took it upon himself to scrounge the mountainsides of Bataan, trudging through the jungles in the dead of night by himself, sometimes behind enemy lines, to look for both herbal medicine and edible plants for his patients at the General Field Hospital. This was done obviously at great risk to himself.

Shortly before the Fall of Bataan, he and some other Filipino officers of the Medical Corps received official orders from Gen Douglas MacArthur to transfer, as non combatants, to the Malinta Tunnel Hospital in Corregidor. He and his fellow doctors were to be picked up by a US naval PT boat at Mariveles and transferred to Corregidor.The navy boat assigned to take him and his medical team from Mariveles to Corregidor was however commandeered at gun point by American enlisted men who were seeking to escape themselves. My father and his fellow Filipino officers were off loaded by the Americans at gun point before they could take off. Lolo Apeng and his fellow doctors were able later to find wooden bancas to take them to Corregidor.

My father referred to that particular group of American soldiers who took the boat assigned to his team at gun point as the "biggest bunch of cowards" he ever met in the War. My father and fellow doctors, all Filipinos, were all commissioned officers in the United States Armed Forces in the Far East (USAFFE). The Americans who ordered my father and his companions off the boat were enlisted men led by a sergeant. The Filipinos clearly outranked the Americans. As the boat pulled away, the sergeant tossed his 45 cal pistol to the Filipinos and insultingly told my father and his fellow doctors, who were all unarmed, to defend themselves with the pistol.

Of course, as doctors, they were technically non combatants. As such, they were not allowed to bear arms under the Geneva Convention. To be caught with a firearm, a doctor could be executed on the spot by the enemy. That is why when my father used to scavenge for medical herbs and food behind enemy lines in the mountains of Bataan, he had to travel without firearms.

Lolo Apeng was eventually captured in Corregidor. He was transferred to the prison camps of Capas, Tarlac, and then the Old Bilibid Prison in Manila. After he was released from there, he traveled to Baguio, where he surreptitiously resumed his medical services for American strugglers and Filipino Guerrillas in the Mountain Province and neighboring provinces.

To get to these provinces, Lolo Apeng travelled through the mountain passes of the town of Malico between the Mountain Province and Nueva Ecija mostly in the dead of night. He would leave our residence in Baguio City sometimes three or four times a month, fetched by mysterious men at night. These men turned out to be guerrillas in the Resistance. More often than not, he would be led by the guerrillas towards the town of Malico. It is notable that Malico was used for passage by both the Resistance and the Japanese troops seeking passage to other provinces. Each of those treks of Lolo Apeng were obviously extremely dangerous.

Eventually, Lolo Apeng was captured, imprisoned and severely tortured by the Japanese Kempetai for these activities. The person who turned in my father was our Japanese gardener who had been in the employ of my family for 15 years before the outbreak of WW II. This gardener showed at my parents' house, heading the Japanese arresting party. He was dressed in a full colonel's uniform of the Japanese Army. He was obviously a fifth columnist sent by Japan to the Philippines long before the War.

One of my earliest recollections of Lolo Apeng was when my mother took me to visit him in the Baguio Japanese Kempetai jail. When I saw him, he was hanging by his thumbs with his arms pulled behind his torso and above his head from the prison rafters. His toes barely touched the ground, and he had been beaten to unconsciousness. Nevertheless, Lolo Apeng was released after about two months of severe torture. His Japanese captors could not get him to confess to his guerrilla activities. However, at one time, shortly thereafter, Lolo Apeng and his family, which included me, were lined up by the Japanese in front of a machine gun and threatened with death if he didn't confess. He did not. And we miraculously were released unharmed.

Lolo Apeng survived the imprisonment, the torture and the War. For his efforts, he was awarded after the War the US Prisoner of War Medal by the US Ambassador to the Philippines at the US Embassy in Manila.

Long after the award of the Prisoner of War Medal, Lolo Apeng also received the US Congressional Gold Medal (along with some his fellow Veterans who served with the USAFFE in WW II). This however was sparse recognition from the US for Filipinos who fought and died for the cause of freedom in a War not of their making, and who received nothing in return from their colonial master, the United States.

One thing is noteworthy about my father and his Filipino comrade in arms. Although they were all Filipinos, they served while the Philippines was a colony of the United States. During this colonial period, Filipinos were technically and legally American nationals. Filipino citizens as such were non existent from a legal perspective. Indeed, Filipinos of that era were issued American passports. It is one of the tragedies of Philippine-American relations that Filipino veterans of the USAFFE in WW II were not granted the same benefits and recognition as American veterans who served in the same theater of the War. It is an injustice still waiting to be addressed and corrected even as the last Filipino USAFFE veterans have passed on.

(Raf Evangelista April 15, 2002)

....

21
Haiku Musings x 30

Through Heavy Shoving –

The Elephant

Through heavy shoving,
The elephant in the room
Is ignored by all.

Chat Box

God in a chat box?
Those who advocate A.I.

Might dare to try it.

Precious

A plotful of soil
Lasts much longer than money.
What is more precious?

Unsaid

What we do not say
Can be more beneficial
Than what we do say.

Silence

Move on gracefully.
Try to keep your dignity.
Silence can mean all.

Keep The Flame Alive

Take an ember from
The flame and its glow will die.
Keep the fire burning!

Explanations

Why we should explain:
Explaining requires a heart,
A desire to cure.

To Judge Stop trying to judge.
When you judge you may condemn.
You are not my God!

To Light

Do not be dismayed.

What is done in darkness
Always comes to light.

Not My Way

It can't be "My way, Or no way!"
That is not what Democracy is!

Graffiti

Painted graffiti,
Real art or grotesque paintings?
Who can really say?

Tomorrow?

Could the Ukraine now
Be East Asia tomorrow?
Keep holding your breath!

Segregation

Fight segregation
In whatever shape or form,
Except garbage.

Mayhem
In the cusps of grief,
Mayhem caused by dynasties
Continue to rule.

Dynasties
Dynasties are the
Fruit of the poisonous tree,
Greed of politics.

That What Beats

What for are good looks,

If an evil heart beats in
The depths of the soul?

Why?

If a friend asks you
To sacrifice for his goals,
He must answer why.

Ways To Love
How do I love thee?
Let me count the ways:
Till it hurts! It hurts!

The Itch

Wearing someone's skin
Really isn't that kosher.
You can't scratch the itch.

Peace

Peace is never won
By hate which scorches the earth
And tortures the heart.

Exceeding

God exceeds greatness,
He exceeds expectations,
But then He is God!

The River

I am the River.
Through Me all things will flow.
Know that I am God.

Taking Flight

The eyelids of night
Droop to a close in stillness,
As the moon takes flight.

Hand

A Hand lifts the shade
On the glorious sunshine,
Painting the skies gold.

In My Heart

I found the Lord God!
I searched for Him everywhere.
He was in my heart!

Eyes Speak
There are ways to love
Even without speaking words.
The eyes say so much.

Be Like God
Gentleness is love.
So is patience that listens.
Try to be like God!

Is War Ever Justified?

A heavenly cause
Can also be the devil's curse.
Is war justified?

Music
Music from the sky:
Birds in flight singing to the
Humming of the winds.

God Waits

I know that God waits.
He waits for each one of us
To return to Him.

(Raf Evangelista, 5 March 2023)

....

22
Cory and Noynoy - Democracy By Public Servanthood

On the eve of the anniversary of the People's Power Revolution on February 25, 1986, we may wish to contemplate on the following:

There were significant differences between the presidencies of the two Aquinos and some other presidencies. The circumstances were quite different and extraordinary. And impressively, the two presidencies of Cory and Pnoy were not dynasties at all.

1. There was NO AMBITION. Ninoy was the politician; Cory and children led quiet lives. Simple lives. They lived in Times Street QC, starkly different from the Forbes Park residences of their cousins. Cory was no socialite. Her routine was never that of the blue ladies of lore. She picked up her children in school and was a hands-on mom. The children were low-profile achievers, magagaling pero mapagkumbaba, walang wang-wang.

2. Events unfolded, something that can not be orchestrated by mere mortals or even by the most astute politician. The Powerful miscalculated, the evil of the avaricious ironically unleashed a more powerful force - an awakened people. It was as if a Divine Hand led Cory and PNoy to a place not of their own choosing. But they were the chosen and the anointed to lead.

2. Cory and PNoy did NOT COVET POWER, they were thrust into it. They did not want it; but they and family had to go in deep prayer to discern God's Will, and they came out of it with a willingness to serve.

3. When Cory was in midterm of her presidency, Noynoy approached her about his intention of running as Tarlac congressman. "Not in my term" said Cory. Noynoy did not run. Clearly it was not AMBITION nor POWER-TRIPPING that fueled his desire to serve.

4. After their respective terms, there was an uneventful changing of guard, and they returned to their unassuming abode in Times St. as ordinary citizens.

5. Cory assumed the presidency under a revolutionary government (People Power). She had an option to run a new term but she chose not to. PNoy did not initiate Charter Change or amendments that would have extended his term (unlike FVR, GMA and Du30). They served to the best of their abilities - Cory to restore the democracy that had been hijacked, and PNoy to rebuild the democratic institutions that had been corrupted.

6. They did not enrich themselves while in power. They knew they had a legacy to protect. Beyond that, they literally considered themselves Servants of the People.

If people can not make out what all that was - I'll spell it out ... DEMOCRACY by PUBLIC SERVANTHOOD.

But it is our failing if we did not take cognizance of the suffering, the sacrifice, the hard work the Aquinos went through for our country. Some have demonized them, ridiculed decency, laughed at matuwid na daan. And that's why we are in a shithole now.

And that is our Nation's loss! Raf Evangelista, (A former next door neighbor of the Aquinos On Times St, QC) 23 February 2023

....

23
Kami Ang Bagyo

They cackled, "Kaya nyo Ba ang darating na bagyo?" We answered: "Kami ang bagyo. Kami'y di magpapaloko!"

Cool winds sing and whisper. We gather under rain showers. Watch and pray that Good, not Evil, will be arriving soon after.

There are good storms after all, All who thirst will come to realize. Good to dry, starving fields below, We come to plant, to fertilize.

The goodness of God's rain Will bring singing to dry streams, Green cover to leafless trees, Drizzles to subdued sunbeams.

Rainbows will cross our land And birds will sing and fly Freely among rain showers Sent down from God's sky.

Be ready for the People. They are the brewing storm That will bring the rainbows. We are the coming norm.

"Kami ang bagyo na padating. Dala nami ang hanging amihan. Huwag matakot at magatubili. We are the good storm, kabayan."

Kami ay makabayan tao, Katarungan ang alay sa inyo! (Raffy Evangelista, 10 November 2021)

....

24
Holes Fit For Roses

Flowers are usually used to represent love. The heart in this poem, despite the hurts, symbolized by the holes, continues to love, and each hole is filled with a rose (REE)

Holes Fit for Roses

My heart is imperfect,
Full of holes and hurting,
Stretching out to others
In deep hopes of loving.

No two holes the same,
A heart filled with light,
And only pure roses
That fit each hole right.

Relationships I built
Form the fabric of life,
But distance in any form
Cuts sharp like a knife.

To love is to know,
To know is to hold.
I will cherish those loved
Till I have grown old.

It wasn't really my dream,
But it is still fine with me
To have a heart full of holes,
Filled with roses I see.

(Raf Evangelista 23 September 2021)

....

25
POLITICAL DYNASTIES

With the current dispensation in power, albeit a continuation of power of one family that held power for so long, should we again be forewarned about:

POLITICAL DYNASTIES

Political Dynasties Are A Bane To Our Democracy And Are Inherently Contrary To The Concept Of The Sovereignty Of The People –

We should not vote for candidates who are members of political dynasties, as the phrase is understood and defined in all legitimate dictionaries.

The tragedy of the anti dynasty bills(s) pending In Congress is that the Legislature wants to define what political dynasties are, but are unwilling to accept the definitions of "dynasty" in established dictionaries.

Political dynasties do not necessarily mean, and should not mean, what Congress says they are, specially if what Congress says is completely askew from dictionary definitions.

The Constituticn bans political dynasties. But the Supreme Court has ruled that this provision is not self implementing and the phrase "political dynasty" needs to be defined by law. An unfortunate appendage from my point of view to Supreme Court's ruling. As a result, some Philippine lawmakers are "eyeing a way to water down any anti-political dynasty bills pending in Congress."

Under a pending bill, the proposed dynasty ban covers the spouse, children, sisters and brothers, and grandchildren of an incumbent elective official, whether national or local. A watered down bill proposed in Congress would amend the original bill to allow "two members of a political family to occupy elective posts at the same time."

The compromise is being suggested because the original bill would adversely affect at least a big number of the members of the House of Representatives, by some estimates more than half of its 289 members. Justification for the proposed amendment is that obtaining the support for the pending bill by a majority of the House would be difficult.

The proposed amendment is a clear admission that a majority of the legislators are more interested in serving their self-serving, parochial interests that in fulfilling the clear spirit of the Constitution, which is to bar political dynasties.

The implications of this proposed amendment to the bill on political dynasties must be scrutinized carefully. An analysis of the amendment would arguably show that the proposal encourages, rather than discourages, allows rather than prohibits, the establishment of political dynasties in the Philippines.

The problem with the suggested compromise is that the solution flies in the face of what should be, and is, the common understanding, and the textbook/dictionary meaning, of the word "dynasty."

Under the proposal, an unlimited succession of elective officials from the same political family can occupy elective positions as long as the number does not exceed two. This would allow the political family to foist any two of their family members ad infinitum over generations, provided the number of family members at any time does not exceed two. It is mind boggling that the proponents do not see that their amendment would in fact be a license for political dynasties to proliferate.

When the Supreme Court declared that Congress must pass an enabling law that would define what a "political dynasty" means, it goes against the grain, intellectually and emotionally, for this to be interpreted to mean that Congress can ascribe a meaning to the word "dynasty" which is contrary to the traditional and time accepted textbook/dictionary meaning of the word.

After all when the Constitution prescribes the respect for human rights, and Congress is asked to define what "human rights" are, Congress has no mandate or authority to redefine what or who "human" is. "Human" is "human" as defined by Oxford, Webster and Colliers, regardless of color, creed or standing in life.

Webster's Third Int'l Dictionary defines "dynasty" as "a succession of rulers of the same line of descent." Again, the controversial proposed amendment would allow for political families to establish dynasties, although the number of elective positions they could hold would be limited to two at any given time. Clearly, it would "allow a succession of rulers of the same line of descent."

Moreover, standard definitions of the word "dynasty" are not limited to a succession of leaders from one family. Webster's Third Int'l Dictionary also defines the word as: 2 a: a group or class of individuals having power or authority in some sphere of activity and able to choose their successors, b: a family that establishes and maintains predominance in a particular field of endeavor for generations.

The Random House Dictionary defines "dynasty" to mean: 3. A series of members of a family who are distinguished in their success, wealth, etc.

The Funk & Wagnals Standard Dictionary, Int'l Edition, also defines "dynasty" to mean the length of time during which one family is in power.

The proposed amencment thus far runs afoul of all these dictionary definitions of the word "dynasty," and no amount of hyperventilating postulations by members of Congress can validly change these definitions.

When the Supreme Court ruled that the Constitutional ban on Political Dynasties is not self implementing and that there is need for an enabling legislation, the Court could have only envisioned a law that would define to what civil degree of consanguinity, starting with the first degree onward to the fourth degree of consanguinity, the prohibition against political dynasties would apply.

To construe the Supreme Court ruling in any other way could lead to the illogical and undesireable conclusion that politicians and their kin may claim proprietary rights to the positions of power that they currently hold. Power in perpetuity is not the name of the game in a Democracy.

Any other definition of "Political Dynasty" would necessarily have to be construed as a questionable license, albeit a judicially abetted one, for Congress to redefine the dictionary (and common sense) meaning of the word "Dynasty." Raffy Evangelista 2022

....

26
Living With Joy, And Being A Man For Others

One can count his age and consider the total days and years as his compendium of life. But life means much more. Life is a myriad of teachings and learnings. It is a tale of life-changing lessons with a touch of laughter and happiness, and a touch of tears and sadness. The jokes and sad tales shared with others are mirrors of reality. But the humor and joy that come with life makes us realize that one can maintain positivity in any situation. Ultimately, life successfully spent is about dwelling on the smiles and laughter, while learning from the frowns and tears. Life is about focusing on kindness and selflessness, rather than personal gain and greed.

Through it all, the best thing that we must learn is that focusing and dwelling on the sad and ugly things as a disgruntled bystander in the corner is no way to live life. One must dream dreams, aim high, take risks, be bold, all for the sake of joyous righteousness. Risk-taking for good is not an impulsive act but rather an act of deliberately trying and learning, and thus becoming a better version of oneself. And in this process, one will understand that life is best Spirit led. This is what ultimately brings true joy, peace and good humor. This is what life should be all about – reveling in the joy of being a Man For God And Others. (Raffy Evangelista, 11 September 2022)

....

27
A Forward Look In The Winter of My Life

It sounds so ridiculous for me to worry about the future of a guy on his 82nd birthday. Worry, almost like subtle fear, should have no place in the life of an octogenarian. There is a very thin line between worry and fear, although both worry and fear can dangerously slip into each other's turf resulting in confusion and anxiety.

When that happens, I tell myself neither to be afraid nor be worried – I just pray and put my complete trust in the hands of my Creator. Worry is a complete waste of time and energy; worse, it paralyzes one into inaction, and nothing can be more exhausting!

I would like to believe that I care passionately about life – mine and other people's lives, now more than ever, in the winter of my years.

Bear with me if I seem to overreact about matters I care about, but time does seem to run out faster as I grow older. And I am therefore inclined to be more and more selective of the company I keep. With time so precious, I don't want to pretend with someone dear who is also pretending.

Why should I play that game at this stage? I'm liberated by my age from all frivolities and fakeness— and, yes, liberated from fear, too! Oh, that the rest of my life be spent in gratitude and appreciation of all the years of good fortune and good health, along with the priceless lessons learned from pain and loss, and it be spent with friends and family who are the treasures of my life! Have a meal, go malling, watch a show with them as often as time and resources allow.

But then it is surprising and disappointing though how some younger people seem to find little time or need for the closeness of friendship, at a time the elderly need it most. Many seniors, whether rich or in the home for the aged, have been known to express the same sense of abandonment. Worse, there are younger people who prefer not to have the elderly in their lives. For sure, the separation and alienation between the young and the old did not happen overnight, but step by step over a lifetime. We, the older ones, might have been able to turn things around earlier if we cared enough to have acted on it, instead of just smiling and worrying in silence.

The irony is, the loudest lament usually comes from those who sacrificed more than they should have, which, of course, predictably backfires on them. The odds are stacked against the beneficiaries of such goodwill, the young ones who are imbued with a sense of entitlement and self-importance—ever growing up into mature adults.

It's sad but those who suffer most are the elderly who spoiled the young ones. They put themselves always last, and the younger generations are doing the same thing to them. The beauty and the pain of love of the elderly — or any love for that matter—is that it can continue, stripped of pride, unconditionally. An unconditionally loving old person jumps for joy at any sign of being loved back, even if the reciprocation comes only after some obvious compromise.

People and circumstances change, the youth grow up and have their own lives—these are the facts of life. Looking around at the fate of others, one can easily begin to appreciate the uniqueness of one's situation. Like they say, if asked to put our troubles on the same table to compare them with others, we'd grab our own pile back without a second thought. These days it feels great to be younger than somebody else, but I draw inspiration from the company of older people in relatively good health.

There are no longer many of my older friends, but being with this diminishing lot, I am also inspired that I am slowly but surely working my way with love and joy to my 83rd birthday. (Rafael E. Evangelista, 11 December 2022)

....

28
Hold On! Hold On! Hold!

Hold On! Hold on! Hold on!
Stand together, hold on.
The rains are beating,
The winds are flailing.
The sun for now is gone
But we must carry on.
Till stars start shining,
And moon starts beaming,
We all must carry on.
Even if the sun is gone,
We must hold on! Hold on!
Stand together, hold on!

Like a bird nestled in a nest
You are cradled in my arms,
And I protected in yours.
Through the tempest, best
To stand in strength together,
Buffetted by storms, of course
We stand in the dark that gathers.
Withstand the test, no matter.
Hold on! Hold on! Hold on!

In a while the sun that's gone
Will be found around the bend
And soon the rains shall end!

Don't be afraid of the dark
I am here to stand by you.
Beyond the black are stars
And moon, and skies of blue.
And the sun will say hello
To greet us on our way
We will only have to say,
"Today we will stand by you."
And love will shine again
As we round the bend!
Stand by us! Hold on! Hold on!
My country 'tis for thee,
Sweet land of liberty,
That we must hold on to!
Hold on! Hold on!

(Raffy Evangelista, 12 July 2022)

....

29
Summer Solstice

We search for cooling shadows
Amongst the leafless trees,
Brown with blazing sunshine
And the hot summer breeze.

All shade has danced away
Under the stern glare of the sun.
The sweet songs of springtime
Receded, and now are gone.

The waves of migratory birds

That used to circle the skies
With color, chirping and dance,
Have flown on without goodbyes.

We miss the soft muted whispers
Of the evening grassy lands,
And, under star filled skies, the
Gentle waves on ocean sands.

Pray, let us stay with each other
Until flowers bloom once more,
And soothing showers again return
To calm distant restive shores.

There are none to lead but us
Through this hot, sweltering land.
When morning comes to midnight,
I will need your guiding hand.

When the sun begins to set
And the moon rules the skies
I will seek love's cooling breath
And the sweetness of your sighs.

Come walk with me, my darling,
As we hold our hands together.
Let flowers of love bloom again
Past the scorching heat of summer.

(Rafael E Evangelista, 13 May 2021)

....

30
Growing up

I learned that accountability doesn't come with age. In this life, you'll meet a lot of people who seem to be at the right age but aren't aware of accountability. People who only care about a problem when it already affects them. People who, among all, are expected to be mature enough to admit their mistakes and do something about it but do otherwise. In life you'll meet adults who will hold you accountable for their own lapses. And sometimes you have to bear with that.

Because accountability doesn't come with age, it should come with empathy. The ability to put yourself into someone else's shoes and look at life from where they're standing. Accountability should come from empathy because empathy makes you see how your carelessness will affect others. So instead of just sitting comfortably, unbothered by the chaos you know you played a part in, you stop making excuses for yourself and face your truth. You stop trying to negotiate that your intention was good and the outcome wasn't what you wanted. When you have empathy, you learn to take accountability over the consequences of your actions regardless of your intention. (Raffy Evangelista, 25 August 2022)

....

31
SIX ELEMENTS OF A TRUE APOLOGY AND GENUINE REMORSE

Many are not aware of these elements of a true apology. Please teach the children-

SIX ELEMENTS OF A TRUE APOLOGY AND GENUINE REMORSE

1)Expressing REGRET- "I am sorry."

2)Requesting FORGIVENESS - "Please forgive me."

3)Accepting RESPONSIBILITY - "I was wrong." "I accept responsibility for my actions."

4)Making RESTITUTION- "What can I do to make it right?" "I will do everything in my power to make things right and to make you whole!"

5)Genuine RESOLUTION - "I'll not do it again." "I will make sure it never happens again."

6)IMPLEMENTATION ASAP of the first 5 elements - "I will act ASAP on all the first five elements!"

Anything short of this is not true remorse nor a true apology for the wrong done, and is a perversion of true justice. (REE, 6 September 2022)

....

32
Random Thoughts On Contriteness And Redemption-

Guilt And Redemption
Admitting we are wrong
When we are in the wrong
Is not admitting defeat.
It is a sign of strength.

But our admission by itself
Does not ensure redemption.
An admission that a wrong
Occured, but refusing to accept
Responsibility, is not strength.
Rather, it is cowardice.

We must use that confession
Of guilt as the starting point to

Confirm that we are willing
To accept reproof,
To heal hurts,
To right wrongs,
To restore all those who
Have been deprived,
To do justice to all who
Have suffered at our hands,
To distance ourselves from
Vendors of evil and greed.

We must not waste the
Fruits of our admission.
We must restore.
Our admission of wrong
Will only bring healing,
Will only right the wrong,
Will only be our salvation
Precisely if those who have
Been deprived by what
We have wrongfully done,
Are fully restored.

And, as importantly,
if we are to correct the
Wrong and foresake
Our wrongful ways, there
Must be 1) a resolution of
Whatever caused the
Problem in the first place …
And 2) a resolution that the
Wrong will not ever happen
Again. Yes, the wrong doer
Must resolve to do both.

Admission, restitution, resolution
Are our only basis for us to lay
Claim to that final victory of
Righteousness and redemption.

Otherwise evil will continue
To consume us … despite
Any admission.

Such a confession - disclaiming
Guilt, and without restitution
and resolution - is at best an
"Argumentum Ad Misericordiam,"
An Appeal To Pity, and little else.

(REE, 14 August 2022)

Proverbs 1:9/19 –
My son, should sinners entice you, and say,
"Come along with us!" …
Let us lie in wait for the honest man,
let us set a trap … for the innocent,
All kinds of precious wealth shall we gain."

My son, walk not in the way with them …
This is the fate of everyone greedy of loot:
unlawful gain takes away the
life of him who acquires it.

Proverbs 13:18 –
Poverty and shame befall
the man who disregards
correction, but he who
heeds reproof is honored.

....

33
Passive Acceptance Will Not Work In Democracy, Which Is Defined As:

A Government Of, For, And BY THE PEOPLE

A survey was conducted some years ago on how people, specially at Barangay level, understand the 1987 Constitution and the Local Government Code, specially the empowering provisions of both.

The survey revealed that the Local Government Code's provisions were either poorly understood or ignored by officials, while their constituents knew little or nothing about it, not especially their role in the barangay's governing processes.

In almost ten years of supposed implementation, the Local Government Code's intent to expand the democratic space, empower the community, and activate local or economy found no resonance in the consciousness or acts of those surveyed. The structures and processes it prescribed were largely inoperative. At best, the officials simply simulated them in ways that enabled them to manipulate the community and its resources in order to stay in power.

Many too were unaware that the 1987 Consitution mandates that "Sovereignty resides in the People, and that all governmental authority emanates from them." Far less were aware of the Local Government Code grants to the residents of each Barangay, acting collectively as a Barangay Assembly, the power to be the supreme governing body in the Barangay, in fulfillment of the mandate of the Constitution.

Field verification and analyses of the findings led to the conclusion that neither autonomy nor democracy had advanced to any significance. Quite the contrary, it regressed as money became the driving force of grassroots politics. The introduction of the internal revenue allotment (IRA) for local governments, coupled with the ballooning of congressional pork barrel allowances, fueled the use of patronage as an instrument of political control on all levels. This enabled family dynasties to dominate politics as never before -- on all levels starting with the barangays.

With the rise of money politics, governance of the feudal variety came alive with a vengeance. Traditional politics produced trapos and trapo governance became the vogue. Contrary to the Code's intent to decentralize power and empower the people, trapo leaders became even more powerful and in firmer control of the grassroots. With patronage and paternalism in full bloom, it was no surprise that elections favored them, turning barangay constituencies into fiefdoms ruled by family dynasties that in turn owed their allegiance to Big Bosses at municipal, provincial and national levels.

Why this happened despite the empowering provisions of the Local Government Code could be ascribed to two reasons. When it became law: a) the trapos, back in office soon after EDSA I, simply ignored its transparency and accountability provisions, and b) no one bothered to inform the people of the Code's provisions – especially of their mandated role in local governance.

For instance, people were not informed that the Code had set huge allocations to their barangay government – for operations and for capitalizing local development. Nor were they informed that they had a say in how these were to be spent. They didn't know that they now had direct charge of their community's affairs -- as members of the Barangay Assembly, the local parliament. They didn't know they had the power of Recall, that they could actually remove or replace abusive or corrupt officials. Nor were they told of their right of Initiative and Referendum, whereby they could directly initiate legislation or nullify undesirable ordinances.

What was so disappointing about the survey's revelations was that no one -- not even the interior and local government department -- bothered to undertake an information campaign on its new and empowering provisions. Thus, uninformed, kept in the dark, the people remained powerless while the trapos who were already in power feasted on their powerlessness and became more powerful. Local autonomy remained a pipe-dream, as did local development despite the billions flowing to the barangays year after year.

Keeping the people in the dark and uninvolved served the trapos well. They could carry on as if the Code had changed nothing of the old system, and stay in power ad infinitum. It didn't help that the putative bebeficiaries of the Code, the 42,000 barangays in the country, did nothing to propagate its provisions and claim ownership of the democracy promised by the Constitution and the Code.

Should the Local Government Code be scrapped? Is the Code an unqualified failure?

The answer to both questions is a resounding "No!"

EDSA I was not supposed to be the end all and be all of the Revolution. That was merely the initial step. Nor was it supposed to culminate with passage of the 1987 Constitution and implementing laws like the Local Government Code. That was the second step. The third step was to educate nationwide the people about their sovereign right to govern the country under the 1987 Constitution and the Local Government Code. The fourth and final step was for the people to enforce their sovereign right and actively rule and govern their respective Barangays through their Barangay Assemblies. These last and final steps still have to be pursued and implemented for People Power to finally succeed.

Government is everybody's business. You cannot expect good governance if you're not involved! (Raffy Evangelista 25 Febuary 2022)

....

34
Our Choice to Make – The coming elections

I wrote this piece in June 2021 with the 2022 national elections in mind. The 2022 elections have come and gone. A question we must start asking ourselves: Did we make the right choice? –

Our Choice To Make: The Coming Elections

It is possible that the forthcoming elections of August 2022 shall represent a choice that each one of us will have to make - a choice between democracy and dictatorship.

The basic difference between a democracy and a dictatorship comes down to means and ends. Democracy is about means, and not just ends. If we all agreed on the ends—such as whether to resort to EJKs in the pursuit of a drug war—there'd be no need for democracy. But of course we don't agree, which is why the means by which we resolve our differences are so important. Those means include a Constitution, a system of government based on the rule of law passed by an independent legislature, interpreted by an independent judiciary, and implemented by an executive branch, working together under the principle of separation of powers.

A dictatorship, by contrast, is only about ends. Those ends are the goals of the dictator—at a minimum, preserving and accumulating personal power. To achieve those ends, a dictator will use any means necessary.

Which brings us to Du30. The conventional criticism of Du30 is that he is unfit to be president because he continuously breaks the norms of how a president should behave.

Du30's norm-breaking is unsettling, to be sure, but Du30's more fundamental offense is he continuously sacrifices means in order to preserve and centralize personal power, often in violation of the principle of separation of powers. He thereby violates a president's core responsibility to protect traditional democracy.

A president who slams and ridicules God and religion in order to get his way on a controversial issue, such as his drug war and EJKs, and threatening to kill religious leaders critical of that drug war, is not protecting the means of democracy. He is treating the government of the Philippines as a bargaining chip. He is asserting power by any means possible. This is the method of a bully and a dictator. A president who claims he has an absolute right to declare a national emergency and spend government funds that Congress has explicitly refused to appropriate for the ends he seeks is also assuming the role of a dictator.

A president who spouts lies during a prime-time national television address over what he terms an "undeniable crisis" that the Church and its prelates are unduely critical of his drug war, which is in fact no crisis at all, is using whatever means available to him to preserve and build his base of power.

In fact, the greatest threats to the Philippines do not come from Du30's critics. The main threats are coming Malacanang itself, and from a foreign government, China, intent on undermining our democracy by propagating lies, turning Filipinos against each other, and shoring up a non-republican president.

There is great concern whether Du30 is actually colluding with China's President Xi to establishing a "Greater China Co-Prosperity Sphere" in the South China Sea, echoes of what Imperial Japan tried to do during WW II. But his willingness to let Xi and China have their way with nary a protest is disconcerting. What we do know so far is that Du30 himself, and his aides, specially his presidential spokesman, actively excuse and justify China's intrusions and incursions into our territory almost at every turn.

We know that since he was elected Du30 has done little or nothing to stop China from impinging and encroaching on our territorial integrity. On the contrary, Du30 has encouraged China's imperialistic ambitions by wheeling and dealing with China and speaking about joint exploration ventures with China of the West Philippine Sea.

The overall pattern is clear to anyone who cares to see it. Du30's entire presidency to date has sacrificed the means of democracy to the end of preserving his personal power. Interestingly enough, he is reported to have claimed that China will not tolerate any attempt to strip him from power.

He has attacked the religion of a majority of Filipinos, the Pope, the International Commission on Human Rights; he has called for the killing of bishops; he lashed out at a Chief Justice who has disagreed him with the goal of stirring up the public against her; encouraged followers to believe that his arch critic, Leila de Lima in the 2016 election should be imprisoned; and he has condemned as "enemies," journalists who report unfavorably about him, in an effort to fuel public resentment – perhaps even violence – against them. He is constantly making gratuitous statements, only to call them jokes. Jokes? Calling them lies and threats would seem more appropos.

To argue, as some Du30 apologists do, that whatever the President does is justified because voters put him in power, is to claim that a dictatorship is justifiable even in a democracy. They cannot. Even if a majority of Filipinos were to attempt such thing (and, remember, Du30 was not voted in by a majority of all Filipino voters in 2016,) the Constitution prohibits it. The choice could not be clearer. Democracy is about means. Dictatorship is about ends. Du30 uses any means available to achieve his own ends.

We can preserve our democracy by voting for the pro democracy candidates in future elections. We can also continue to struggle against someone who strives to thwart democracy for his own benefit.

Democracy is more than just a choice! (REE, 3 June 2021) ……………………

35
Now I Am Building

Now I am building for eternity
Stone by stone upon stone.
Everything a matter of time,
With time swiftly ticking away.

I will try to lay foundations for
Those who will tread after me.
I know I must because I must.
I do not control my tomorrow.

And tomorrow may never come
For me, but it will come for them.
And I can help them with theirs.
Bless the children who play,

Who run, who weep, who laugh,
Bless children who hunger for Love,
And those who thirst for life.
I will help them on this train of

Life that they are just getting on
And I will soon be getting off.
Someday may not exist in my
Tomorrow, for who knows what

God has ordained for my eternity.
There is only the here and now,
At least for me, as the seconds
Even now slowly tick away.

Because there is no "was" or
"Then," but only "now" for me.

(REE, 6 August 2022)

....

36

Decadence of Philippine Democracy

Perhaps in a democracy the distinctive feature of decadence is not debauchery but terminal self-absorption— the loss of the capacity for collective action, the loss of belief in common purpose, even the loss of acceptance of a common form of reasoning.

A decadent elite licenses degraded behavior, and a debased public chooses its worst leaders. Then their Chosen Leader panders to their worst attributes — and they reward him for doing so.

"Decadence," in short, describes a cultural, moral, and spiritual disorder — now represented by some of our recent leaders - within this decadent elite. Six years' worth of Du30's cynicism, selfishness, and rage as President has only stoked the decadent appetite of his supporters. And so they recently elected his replacement, BBM.

Of course Du30 legitimized the language of xenophobia and misogyny even during his campaign for the Presidency. But he has also legitimized the language of cruelty, selfishness and narcissism since he ascended to power.

Filipinos elected the man who had uttered words of vulgarity, sexism, and cruelty with demonic glee. Voters then saw, and his supporters still see, his cruelty and naked self-aggrandizement as signs of steely determination, no matter that Du30 himself sometimes apologizes, with a wan smile or a twisted sneer, for his own bloopers.

Perhaps we can measure democratic decadence by the diminishing relevance of the word "We" in our present society. It is, after all, a premise of democratic politics that, while majorities choose, they do so in the name of collective good.

Not so in the 2016 Presidential elections, and the years after. The fanatical voters who elected Du30 into the Presidency then, and his rabid followers now, did not and do not support Du30 for the sake of the collective good. They do so in the diminished sense of the word "we" - "we" against Ninoy and Cory (long dead before Du30's ascendancy), their son, PNoy, their follower Yellows, the European Union, the United Nations, the Kuwait Government, the Church, the human rights organizations, Obama, de Lima, Sereno, Trillanes, and any one who dares criticize Du30.

This "Decadent We"even supported Du30 when he railed against the Pope. But this democratic decadence reached its peak when this "Decadent We" approved, applauded, and laughed with glee as Du30 blasphemed against the God worshipped by 80% of all Filipinos! And so this "We" has recently elected BBM, the son of our one and only dictator in our Nation's history.

"We", the "Real We" is US, the Filipino People, not them, the "decadent we."Collectively, the "Real We" are the Sovereign. All governmental authoritiy emanates from us. The President and his minions in government are public servants meant to do our collective will, not the will of one man.

The deafening question that remains unanswered after the 2022 national elections is: Was BBM elected by the "Real We" or the "Decadent We?" (REE, 24 July 2020)

....

37

SPINNING WORLD

*Our earth is spinning
In dizzying cycles.
This home we're in
Turns in viral circles.*

*Day in, day out,
Where are we going?
Beyond the turnabouts,
Wild winds are blowing.*

*Turning and turning,
 Blowing to a spining spin.
Man stumbling, fleeing,
In and out, and out and in.*

*No longer rhyme nor
Reason to frenetic turns,
Unmindful of scraping, falling
And those painful burns.*

*Dizzying, dizzying, dizzying.
How, where, and when to go?
Here to there, anywhere,
The virus frightens so!*

*To some the virus is not here.
If so, what then is false or true?
Who then is to ask: who lies?
Is it us, or is it really you?*

*A lie? A farce? The circle
Turns, and truth to tell,
The virus is really here,
And it was born in hell.*

Perhaps to flow, to slide

With viral tides is best.
But will we then survive
This lonely, final test?

Many are embattled,
Many can't eat or sleep.
Viral fears gather
In the circling deep.

The world is spinning
Bewilderingly so.
We need to hold on, till
We know where to go.

(Raffy Evangelista 26 June 2021)

(A lot of people are bewildered, lost and depressed by savage onslaught of the Omicron virus. And the effects psychologically may scar them for a long time. I published this poem to air their plight.)

....

38
Revelation: The Shaking

Let the dark night come.
Let the stars disappear.
I will still have God's dawn
To calm my deepest fear.
Let the strong rains fall.
Let dark clouds billow.
The sun will surely shine
To drown the deepest sorrow.

Where do I go from here?
I search for a place to rest,
I ask Heaven to dry my tears.

Lord, do not put me to the test.
God, please never desert me.
I truly trust in Your great love.
Through darkness that I see,
Please guide me from above.

Lands now shake and tremble.
Shaking comes from nature too.
Will the world now disassemble?
I turn my loving gaze to You.
Do we have the right to even ask
For Your saving grace, O Lord,
When our sins bring us to task
For bearing the devil's sword?

You are Shepherd and Saviour.
You, Jesus, are my Lord and King.
Do not shut Heaven's saving door
On this poor supplicant who sings
This lament about his many sins,
And begs for Your forgiveness,
As Tribulation comes in the din
Of the shaking and darkness.

I believe Jesus that You are God
Who loves and comes to save
Saints, sinners, good and bad.
Repentance is key for He gave
His life long ago upon the tree,
To save us and share His kingdom
For who ever His followers may be.
Repent! May His kingdom come!

I feel, Lord, your warming embrace
Through restless winds of war,
I feel Your love and try to brace
From shakings both here and far.
I surrender to Your loving care
In the turmoil that stirs the heart.

To venture on my own I do not dare,
Be with me as the shakings start.

(Raf Evangelista, 2023)

....

39
The Echo Of The Spoken Word

How the spoken word echoes and resonates depends not only on what, but also when and where the words are spoken. In an empty chamber, words mean nothing, say nothing, and come to nothing. It is different when a message of love, giving and forgiving comes from the chambers of the heart, and is addressed, heart to heart, to one in need of compassion, respect and understanding. Raf Evangelista 7 May 2023

....

40
Our Pledge, The Whimpering Of No Hope, And Defenestration

President Duterte, in his fourth State of the Nation address (SONA), categorically claimed that "The West Philippine Sea is ours. No if and buts. It is ours."

But in almost in the same breath he said "he pleaded with Chinese President Xi Jinping that the Philippines be allowed to fish in waters that form part of its exclusive economic zone," adding that ... "we have to temper it with the times and the realities that we face today."

He also stated that he told him (President Xi) "to please allow us (to fish) because before they were driving away our fishermen."

He reiterated his oft-repeated claim that "If I send my marines ... I guarantee you not one of them will come home alive."

It is noteworthy that his acolytes, Including some newly elected ones, echo the same filiality to China.

Fishermen groups have criticized Du30's remarks, stating "We are dismayed by the usual dichotomizing of our legitimate call for fishing rights and having a war with China ... We can have that sans armed confrontation, only political will ... Now more than ever is the high time to resolve this dispute in the name of preserving our remaining resources."

Surveys have shown that a large majority of Filipinos want Philippine rights over the West Philippine Sea preserved and protected. Despite this, the President has ignored this demand, and has said preciously little about what he is doing to preserve those rights. Except that he has an agreement with President Xi allowing China to fish and explore our waters, and that "he as pleaded with Xi to allow Filipinos to fish in them."

If we will not protect our rights now, as Duterte insists we shouldn't or can't, the question is when? The Philippines can never hope to match the military might of a colossus like China. But there are, as some have pointed out, non-military options that still have to be explored and utilized to assert our rights. The bullying tactics of China is no reason now for the Philippines to slink away, tail between the legs, like a whimpering dog, without any hope.

Have you heard of the word "defenestration?" Many haven't. Many more don't know what it means.

Defenestration is a process that we as a People and a Nation should be concerned about. It means to "throw out the window." It can be meant literally or figuratively. Either way, remember that we needed to do some defenestration during the past national elections.

Whether defenestration happened in the recent elections is of course still a contentious issue.

But the demands of defenestrarion during the last elections included the following - No more corruption, no more incompetence, no more self serving politics! There were cries of - "No" to historical revisionism! Say "No" to populism and authoritarian rule. Say "No" to magnanakaws! And even more basic, no more groveling or whimpering before China and any would be conquerors of or trespassers on our national patrimony and territory.

Surely, we need Servant Leaders, leaders who will act forcefully upon these legitimate demands of the People. Such Servant Leaders are living reminders of a pledge they all make, a commitment we all undertake, for our Flag and Country.

I ask you: do we sing or recite these words that follow … and mean them? The words constitute a Pledge. We should not sing or recite them if we do not mean them! Then ask yourselves: Do our preferred leaders believe in and observe this Pledge? –

Lupang hinirang,
Duyan ka ng magiting!
Chosen land,
Cradle of the brave!
Sa manlulupig,
Di ka pasisiil!
Let no conqueror
Oppress you!
Aming ligaya na pag
May mangaapi,
Ang mamatay ng
Dahil sa iyo!
It will be our joy,
In the face of
Oppression, to
Give up our
Lives for you!

Read the words of our Pledge carefully - "Sa manlulupig di ka pasisiil!" It matters not if the conqueror or oppressor is foreign or homegrown. Our commitment is to lay down our lives for love of Country, our Duyan ng Magiting, in the fight against ANY oppressor. Our country's history, from Lapulapu, to Rizal, Bonifacio, to our soldiers of WW II who fought the Japanese invaders against all odds, to the People's Revolt against the Marcos dictatorship, to our health workers fighting at the frontlines of the covid pandemic, is full of tales of heroism and patriotism.

No "ifs and buts!" No whimpering or defeatism from our heroes who we honor today, our Day of Independence!

There are those so called "Leaders" who would betray our Country to domestic oppressors and foreign invaders, even against the express wishes of the People.

To them, I say: They are NOT Servant Leaders!

Again, I stress - The critical task in any national or local elections is not simply the election of leaders, any leaders. We must carefully choose Servant Leaders who can see us through these critical times when our Country's freedom, autonomy and independence are threatened. We need Servant Leaders who will lead us in fulfilling our Pledge to our Country by word, deed and example. And the most basic criteria in choosing our future leaders is to determine their own faithfulness to this Pledge that they, and all of us, make from childhood!

A Servant Leader must always preach AND practice that "power emanates from the ground (the People) up." Not the other way around.

The perfect definition of a true Servant Leader, after all, is one who truly believes in what the Constitution itself proclaims: "Sovereignty resides in the People, and all governmental authority emanates from them."

Oh, and yes, a true Servant Leader will insist on the implementation of the Rule of Law as far as China and our territorial waters are concerned.

Let us DEFENESTRATE now! Let insist that our leaders assure the people that our Democracy, Independence, and Freedom will survive! Happy Independence Day! Raffy Evangelista, 12 June 2022

....

41
A poem on the failed 2022 national elections

Maybe, Again, Finally

Maybe the tip of starlight was truly there.
Maybe it was not a mirage I saw,
despite the darkness of the seas
caused by thirty one million ghosts.

Maybe the tip of the brightness –
the gathering of fifteen
million stars has been awakened.
Maybe this tip will prove to be
a shining beacon for those
still hidden in the dark beyond.

Maybe I can follow this tip of light,
and find my hope again,
find my courage again, and
navigate and find my way
through the frothing and seething waters
To calmer seas somewhere.

Today,
I will follow that light!
Then … Maybe,
Tomorrow!
Someday!
One day!
And then,
Again,
Finally!

(REE, 4 July 2022)

....

42
EDSA, An Unfinished Revolution

Was EdSA a failed revolution? Or rather was it a failed effort on the part of the people to "perform their obligations?"

EDSA was un unfinished, not a failed, revolution. Even if there were some failures along the way. And many of those failures are our responsibility.

I believe that there had to be five stages to complete the EDSA Revolution:

1. The Revolt itself;

2. A new Constitution and implementing laws;

3. Education and involvement of the people in the empowerment process, specially at Barangay level;

4. Election of competent, trustworthy and knowlegeable officials, at Barangay level, who believe in people empowerment; and

5. Establishment of model barangays in various regions of the Philippines. Of these five stages, only the first two have been accomplished.

Why?

A survey some years ago revealed that the People empowerment provisions of the Constitution and implementing laws are ignored or poorly understood by government officials. But worse, their constituents know little or nothing about their obligations, specially their role in the Barangay's governing process. Instead we the people focused on "their rights." Their sense of entitlement cost them dearly. The lack of understanding by the people of their obligations is the main reason why the EDSA Revolution is still unfinished. And to this day, few understand the basic democratic precept of what a "Public Servant" truly means.

....

43
Now I am Building for Eternity

Now I am building for eternity
Stone by stone upon stone.
Everything a matter of time,
With time swiftly ticking away.
I will try to lay foundations for
Those who will tread after me.
I know I must because I must.
I do not control my tomorrow.
And tomorrow may never come
For me, but it will come for them.
And I can help them with theirs.
Bless the children who play,
Who run, who weep, who laugh,
Bless children who hunger for
Love, And those who thirst for life.
I will help them on this train of
Life that they are just getting on
And I will soon be getting off.
Someday may not exist in my
Tomorrow, for who knows what
God has ordained for my eternity.
There is only the here and now,

*At least for me, as the seconds
Even now slowly tick away.
Because there is no "was" or
"Then," but only "now" for me.*

(REE, 6 August 2022)

....

44
The Confetti Rallies Of Makati

Can we learn something from the Makati Confetti Rallies of 1986? –

The Confetti Rallies of Makati, The Business Revolt Of 1986

Various stories have been circulating over the years regarding the origins of the "Yellow Confetti Rallies" that galvanized the business community in Makati after Ninoy Aquino's assassination on August 21, 1983. These confetti rallies ended in 1986, the year that Ferdinand Marcos fled the country. Confetti rallies in other parts of the country, particularly Cebu and Davao, replicated the Makati experience during that period.

One such story attributes the Makati rallies to the late Sen Butz Aquino and to ATOM. This story states, "As a street parliamentarian, Butz was the 'pasimuno' of the EDSA People's Power Revolution of 1986 when he led the August 21 Movement (ATOM) then raining yellow confetti from Makati's high rise buildings."

Without discrediting Butz Aquino, who indeed played a most important role in the phenomenon of what is now called the EDSA People's Power Revolution, this story should be clarified. This story could lead readers to believe that it was ATOM, Butz's organization, that was responsible for yellow confetti coming from Makati's high rise buildings that led to the protest that "washed away the dictatorship."

Another story is that the confetti rallies were a spontaneous reaction among the Makati denizens to the excesses of Marcos, a story that scratches only the surface of what really transpired. There was indeed some spontaneous combustion in Makati, but not in the simplistic way narrated in this story.

Truth to tell, neither Butz nor Atom had anything to do with the organization of the "yellow confetti" revolt of the business sector, except as participants in the marches that ensued as a consequence of the confetti storm that enveloped the environs of Ayala Avenue.

The confetti rallies of Makati were the brainchild of eight persons who wanted to mobilize the business community immediately after the assassination of Ninoy Aquino. These eight had agonized for months after Ninoy's assassination on what they could do to show their solidarity with Ninoy's cause. Of the eight members, two have since passed on.

The group had been meeting secretly in the back rooms of Makati every Monday, (hence, the name they gave to themselves, "The Monday Group"), to discuss how they could possibly help end the reign of the conjugal dictatorship . One day, in one flash of momentary genius, the group agreed that since the Filipino loves fiestas, they would go the confetti route to mobilize the business community. The idea of organizing confetti rallies proved to be a brilliant one.

The mobilization of the rallies took painstaking and surreptitious implementation. An organizer for each major building along the "Triangle" formed by Ayala, Paseo de Roxas and Makati Avenues had to be located. Sworn to secrecy, the organizers were tasked to mobilize the employees, and, where possible, the employers, in the buildings where they worked.

The instructions to those conscripted were simple: "Wait for an explosion (from a big firecracker called

"Bawang" that would be exploded midway up Ayala Ave), drop confetti (preferably yellow) from your offices, go down and gather on Ayala Avenue." The employees were of course informed that the rallies were to be in protest of the assassination of Ninoy, and would have an anti-Marcos drift.

Marchers from other parts of Metro Manila were also mobilized to converge on the Ayala "Triangle." In subsequent confetti rallies, known critics of the administration and other personalities from the opposition were invited to speak to the gatherings.

Aside from the idea of confetti fiestas, the other stroke of genius was when the Monday Group concluded that it would be difficult to keep the marchers converging in the Makati "Triangle" in place for very long, unless there was a "glue" to hold the crowds. The marchers, tired and thirsty after their marches, would tend to drift away at the end of the marches, even with the best of speakers on hand to address the crowds. To fill up the "Triangle" through the working hours, the Monday Group realized that the Makati employees could provide the needed glue. It became clear that committed employees, who were not exhausted by the marches, could stay for the duration of the rallies. For other employees, of course, the confetti rallies provided them the opportunity to play hooky from work. In fairness though, many employers/bosses were willing conspirators and participants in the rallies themselves with their employees.

(In retrospect, none of the rallies during the so called "EDSA 2" had this "glue," which accounted for why most of the marches of EDSA 2 quickly dissipated after the marchers reached their destination points in Makati.)

The plan for the confetti rallies in Makati worked to perfection. The Makati "Triangle," in the first confetti rally on a specified Friday, exploded in a shower of yellow confetti as large crowds came down from Makati office buildings. It was the start of the business revolt that could not thereafter be stopped. In what seemed like a spontaneous combustion, this confetti rally ignited other regular Friday rallies that lasted and spread until Marcos fled in 1986.

People who were not part of the original organized rally groups started to join the Makati rallies, thousands at a time. Employees started on their own initiative to cut up their PLDT yellow pages into confetti that was showered over Makati during every rally. The anti-Marcos mindset in Makati took on a death challenging life of its own. Even when MetroCom troops entered the Triangle the day after, the employees were not to be deterred. They took to the roof-decks and rained pick-up missiles against the hapless troops. And when Makati Mayor Nemesio Yabut tried to hold his own pro-Marcos rally at the junction of Ayala and Paseo de Roxas, Yabut and his "hakot" crowds were subjected to much the same treatment as the Metrocom troops from the Makati rooftops.

Today, the so called revolt of the business community against the Dictatorship is attributed by many to the yellow confetti rallies of Makati.

The Monday Group have never spoken about their organizing role of the Makati confetti rallies before today. But in the interest of truth on how the confetti rallies started, we have finally decided to tell our story.

In memory of the Monday Group:

By Rafael "Raffy" E. Evangelista Member of the Monday Group, 24 February 2016

....

45
Random Thoughts On Contriteness And Redemption

Guilt And Redemption

Admitting we are wrong
When we are in the wrong
Is not admitting defeat.
It is a sign of strength.

But our admission by itself Does not ensure redemption. An admission that a wrong Occured, but refusing to accept Responsibility, is not strength. Rather, it is cowardice. We must use that confession Of guilt as the starting point to Confirm that we are willing To accept reproof, To heal hurts, To right wrongs, To restore all those who Have been deprived, To do justice to all who Have suffered at our hands, To distance ourselves from Vendors of evil and greed.

We must not waste the Fruits of our admission.

We must restore. Our admission of wrong Will only bring healing, Will only right the wrong, Will only be our salvation Precisely if those who have Been deprived by what We have wrongfully done, Are fully restored.

And, as importantly, if we are to correct the Wrong and foresake Our wrongful ways, there Must be

1) a resolution of Whatever caused the Problem in the first place …

And 2) a resolution that the Wrong will not ever happen Again. Yes, the wrong doer Must resolve to do both.

Admission, restitution, resolution Are our only basis for us to lay Claim to that final victory of Righteousness and redemption.

Otherwise evil will continue To consume us … despite Any admission. Such a confession - disclaiming Guilt, and without restitution and resolution - is at best an "Argumentum Ad Misericordiam," An Appeal To Pity, and little else.

(REE, 14 August 2022)

Proverbs 1:9/19 - My son, should sinners entice you, and say,

"Come along with us!" … Let us
lie in wait for the honest man,
let us set a trap … for

the innocent,
 All kinds of precious wealth shall we gain."
My son, walk not in the way with them …
This is the fate of everyone greedy of loot:
unlawful gain takes away the life of
him who acquires it.

Proverbs 13:18 - Poverty and shame befall the man who disregards correction, but he who heeds reproof is honored.

....

46
Sky Dance

The magnificent red sky joins
The orange sun in a fiery kiss,
Amidst gathering dark of night.
Locked in passionate embrace,
The lovers meld sensually to
The rythmn of swaying winds
That caress heaven's dance.
Silver stars, like fireflies, emerge
To encourage the two lovers on.
In one final, lingering burst of light.
As quickly as it began, the dance
Ends, and the sky,
donning its Purple robes,
gathers the crimson
Sun into its bosom.
In one final Embrace,
 the lovers slide over
The horizon, turn off the lights,
and Bid the day,
"Adieu" in fond farewell.

(Raf Evangelista, 6 May 2023)

....

47
I Weep For The Philippines

Through this COVID 19 pandemic lockdown, media and the internet have been full videos and pictures of the chaotic and overcrowded situations of our urban poor, in Metro Manila and other urban areas of the Philippines. In the sitios, there is little, if no, social distancing, people are hard put to find masks and safety gear. One also has to wonder if they have enough water, much less soap, to wash their hands. We, of the middle and upper echelons of Philippines, simply cluck our tongues in disapproval and ask how some people can be so pasaway!

The tragic conditions of the poor, specially in the sitios of Metro Manila and urban areas, really come into the spotlight in times like now. The pandemic truly underscores how little has been done to alleviate the plight of those who are impoverished and have to live, even in normal times, under impossible conditions. What good is social distancing under COVID 19 if the poor are squashed in together in the places where they live? What good is the stay home rule if the hungry have to go out and beg for their keep.

True leadership does not begin with tirades, threats and bluster. True leadership does not mean a populist leader who dictates according to his own needs and desires. The Philippines needs leadership that listens to and cares for the people, specially the marginalized. We need leaders who recognize that leadership is a privilege, not a right. We need true servant leaders who accept that they are servants first and formost and that real sovereignty resides in the people. The leader of a wolf pack leads mostly from the back of the pack, guiding those who would stray, those who are weak from falling behind and getting lost.

These are times I weep for the Philippines, the land of our people. We tend to blame the Filipino for what we are today. Yes, the Filipino must share some of the blame, because the average Filipino does not understand that Democracy goes beyond the right to vote. The average Filipino does not know that in a true Democracy, it is the people collectively who should lead, not just during elections once every 4 or 6 years but daily, specially at Barangay level where their authority is explicitly recognized by the Constitution and existing laws. Sure, the average Filipino must share some of the blame. But the bulk of the responsibility lies with the wealthier classes and the politicians who have kept the poor in the dark about their true rights and responsibilities.

You and I, and our would-be leaders are the true pasaways! I weep for the Philippines! (REE, 22 April 2020)

....

48
The Torch And The Bridge

I weep for the "Young Once," those who still carry the Torch of Love and Light for our children. We have trudged the long and dusty road of life, often darkened with evil around. And as we approach the end of the Bridge of "Light All Over," we dream of just one thing: to pass on this Torch to our children with the wish and hope that the Torch keeps burning in the hearts of the "Young Ones."

I weep for these "Young Ones." They inherit a torch that sputters because of truth denied and freedom betrayed. Because of machinations of evil ones who block the Bridge of Love and Light, we who would carry the torch foreward are denied access to that bridge. Our Young Ones, too have a singular dream: to accept and carry the torch of love forward to the brightness at the end of the "Bridge of Light All Over."

I now, at 82 years of age, standing at the end of that Bridge, weep for The Young Ones who tread after me. But my hope and faith spring eternal, and I see the "Bridge of Light All Over," looming just beyond the bend. And I Know I will pass on the Torch of Love and of Light to the generations after me! I will continue to fight to my dying breath for the right of the Young Ones to bear the Torch of Love and Light, for the Truth is Worth Living and Dying For!

I am the Young Once, and I now live for those who come after, the Young Ones! I will bless them with the Torch of Eternal Love and Light, and let the Torch lead them through the dangers of the darkness to the "Bridge of Light All Over." (Raffy Evangelista 28 March 2023)

....

49
Dear Politician/Servant Leader (Kuno):

Please Connect The Dots, And Do Not Be Insulted When I ask you to "connect the dots," –

1) I am not making fun of you or belittling you;

2) I am not saying you do not know how to speak or express yourself;

3) I am not saying you do not think or that you are illogical;

4) I am not questioning your intelligence;

5) I am not trying to pin you down on perceived mistakes.

I am simply saying I do not know most times what you are referring to. I am simply telling you that if I am to respond or react to what you say, I have to know what it is I am supposed to be responding or reacting to. By doing so, I am not laying blame on anyone, least of all you.

Think about it, there would simply be a failure of communication between you and the people if no one is allowed to ask for clarification from you. Politicians must not speak disjointedly, should not ramble on and on, and lose track of subjects and predicates. And this, without even considering the lack of central themes and messages.

On the other hand, I admit that if you feel that it is my intention to insult your intelligence or slander your ability to express your ability to speak, you have the perfect right to be insulted. But that is not my intention. Let me assure you, that with me, it is simply a case of a citizen wanting to be clarified on what you, a "Servant of the People"is saying, nothing more, nothing less. At no time do I intend to insult or slander you.

That having been said, I personally think it is better for me to ask you to "connect the dots," than for me not to respond to you at all simply because I do not understand your statement or question.

Which happens lots of time! I believe you know who you are! There may be more than one of you pontificating to the confusion of the People' (REE, 18 April 2023)

....

50
The New Suzerainty

I wrote this in April 2021. It may still be relevant today, with some amendments) –

Suzerainty is a relationship in which one state or other polity controls the foreign policy and relations of a tributary state, while allowing the tributary state to have internal autonomy. The dominant state is called the "suzerain." Suzerainty differs from sovereignty in that the tributary state is technically independent, but enjoys only limited self-rule.

Although the situation has existed in a number of historical empires, it is considered difficult to reconcile with 20th- or 21st-century concepts of international law, in which sovereignty is a binary which either exists or does not. While a sovereign state can agree by treaty to become a protectorate of a stronger power, modern international law does not recognise any way of making this relationship compulsory on the weaker power. Suzerainty is a practical, de facto situation, rather than a legal, de jure one. (Wikipedia)

This is what could happening in our part of the world. China is trying to establish a suzerainty in the Asia Pacifc Region. The obvious intention is for China to be, in the very least, the suzerain or the dominant state in this part of the world. It is trying to exercise control over the foreign policy of the Philippines to the extent of trespassing on Philippines seas, claiming those seas and islands within those seas are China's, and demanding that sea and air passage over the area by other States requires China's permission.

Most Filipinos view the United States as an ally today, even as there seems to be an attempt by some Philippine authorities to create and/or accept a new geopolitical normal cf special relations with Mainland China. China is, I believe, trying to replicate on a grander scale the Japanese plan of a greater Asia under the Japanese Co-Prosperity Sphere. The Philippines had the courage to fight Japan's Imperialism sacrificing over a million Filipino lives to do so. All that sacrifice of lives may go for naught. Sadly, former President Duterte seemed to welcome this attempt by China to establish a new suzerainty. To my mind, the Duterte Government was complicit in this attempt. The present Marcos government is opague on where it stands with China. It seems that Marcos is engaged in the "roll of the dice" game, reaching out in appeasment of our giant neighbor from the north, while playing footsies the our erstwhile ally, the United States.

It was the height of political naïveté for Duterte's Philippines to expect that under China's suzerainty, our country would enjoy the kind of political autonomy that we enjoy today. All that one has to do is to look to the political experience of HongKong and Taiwan with China. China does not endorse real political autonomy, and can and will use draconian measures to retain and increase political, economic, and if need be, military control over a vassal state or territory.

That being the case, do we have to make a choice, as we did at the start of WW II, between two world powers, China or the United States? (Rafael E Evangelista updated 15 April 2023)

....

51
Among Spring Rainbows

Sharing **two love poems** for all who have lost loved ones recently or in the past:

Among Spring Rainbows

A breeze blows through my window.
In the shifting light of the evening star,
The silk curtains sigh and gently flow,
A song of love singing but from afar.

Is that you, my love, in the gentle light
Of the evening sky singing softly to me?
I reach out to catch and touch the sight

Of the star's soft rays I can clearly see.

A night bird coos in the deep shadows
Of needle pines and late winter green,
Coaxing spring blooms to show and grow,
For now in darkness they sleep unseen.

The sky and the woods speak of love
Even as I miss you dearly through the night.
I will search for you among stars above,
And will love you with the coming light.

Wait for me wherever you might be
I will be searching for you in the spring
Beyond the mountains and the sea
To hear the music of your love sing.

I know that you have waited for me
Through all these winter days gone,
Your smile once more I hope to see
Beneath spring rainbows of the sun.

(Raffy Evangelista 18 April 2021)

A Smile In Your Heart

One day I will go on a journey,
To where love always abides.
I shall love you still so dearly,
And forever be at your side.

Even when heaven calls me home,
My vows to you will not be broken.
I promise you I shall never roam,
Even while I journey on to heaven.

I mean to forever share your heart,
And always have you be a part of me,
For God never meant us to be apart,

But for us to be united for all eternity.

Then when heaven becomes my home,
I will wait, and neither grieve or mourn,
For I know that one day you will join me
With the coming of that blessed morn.

I will wait for that blessed day
When we two shall again be one
And you and I can always stay
United under God's Forever Sun.

And when I pass, look after me,
Even if we are physically apart,
Look to where I shall always be,
A smile in the corner of your heart.

(Raffy Evangelista, 15 March 2021)

....

52
Eighty Blessed Years

I belong to the generation of endangered species of eighty year olds. I wrote this poem for all who have reached their iconic 80th birthdays and can almost touch the sky. Just to clarify, I wrote this poem two years ago when I turned 80. –

I have lived for 80 blessed years,
700,800 hours in 80 years of life,
700,800 hours of smiles and tears.
24 hours daily of friendship and strife,
365 days a year of joys and fears.

Celebrations and disappointments,
Come, gone throughout this time

Remind me that all these moments
Have really little reason or rhyme
For the building of monuments.

Things happen in momentary flashes
As can moments happen in measures.
Designed wishes or sudden rushes,
Bring sadness, and others, treasures,
Of heavenly flight or sudden crashes.

I have had my own share of laughter
And, even with my loved ones, tears.
The chattering, the joking and banter
Throughout these 80 blessed years ...
And loves broken and ripped asunder.

Despite all this, and maybe because,
I shall never trade my age of eighty,
80 years of love's sweet sour sauce,
Beyond the sugar of forty or of fifty.
To return to thirty, no reason or cause.

I have reached the age of 80 years,
I never realized that I ever would.
I was filled when younger with fears
If I would reach fifty, or ever could,
But I reached 80 despite many tears.

Who should I really thank that 80 I did:
You, you, or you, friend or foe or both?
Who among you would care to even bid
That within old bones as mine is growth
Of love, hope ground fine by life's grid?

Shall I celebrate these 80 blessed years,
700,800 love hours in 80 years of life,
80 and 700,800 of smiles and cheers,
Of broken hearts, promises and strife
80 filled years despite fears and tears?

I, born of God's grace, choose 10 x 8!
And I Will Celebrate!
Lord, help me Celebrate!

(Rafael E Evangelista 15 April 2023)

....

53
Way Home

No raindrop falls
in the wrong place.
Each star in heaven
is where it is meant to be.
Every rain drop will surely
end up in the sea, even as it
Falls on the shore.
I swim in vast oceans with the tides
so I can fly with rainbows that
rain has formed among the clouds.
Tall mountains show me the sky,
so I can reach out and touch
the face of heaven. I walk
the earth in order find my path.
And so I follow the last river
that runs to the sea, and
as the final drop of rain flows
to God's ocean,
I am flying home.

(Raf Evangelista, 26 March 2023)

....

54

GOVERNANCE OF ENLIGHTENED AND REAPONSIBLE CITIZENRY

As Distinguished from GOVERNANCE OF LEADERSHIP- A large segment of our population elect leaders and support them on the basis of the perception that they are strong leaders who promise change, a change the people so desperately want. This is a choice of governance based on leadership, which I call a GOVERNANCE OF LEADERSHIP. The voters choose on the basis of their perception that this man or that man is a strong leader who will bring about the change they want.

There is nothing wrong with electing strong leaders. But a democratic state needs more than just governance of leadership.

The historical experience from this system of governance is that strong leadership alone has led to populist, autocratic regimes (the regimes of Stalin, Hitler, Mao Tse Tung, Pol Pot, Abu Bkr Albagdadi of ISIS to name a few) that have abused their centralized power, including favoring those who believe and support these leaders over the rest of the population. That is in fact how these leaders remain in power- by supporting a few, eg. army generals, who in turn will assure the army's support for the leaders.

One of the most important things to learn from the history of mankind is that the masses will easily follow a madman if they are struggling and the madman promises a better life. This is a very scary attribute about human nature, but it is unfortunately true. People who have been struggling for an extended amount of time are easy prey for dynamic leaders – even if the leaders are horrible human beings. The promise of a much better life is like a drug that can hypnotize the masses.

Governance based on leadership alone seldom leads to the success of Lee Kwan Yu of Singapore. Lee, although he established a strong man rule in his country, was in fact blessed to have a strong and informed citizenry ahead and behind him. The success of leadership by strong men alone is more the exception than the rule. As the failed regimes of Hitler, Stalin, Mao Tse Tung and Pol Pot prove, centralized power tends to be abused over time. The key then to a successful democracy is not a strong, centralized system of governance by leadership.

To succeed, a political system must have a broader base, what I call GOVERNANCE OF GOOD CITIZENSHP. An informed, involved, committed and dedicated citizenry - a true government of, for, and by the people - must be the true source of governance.

And this must mean more than simply the power to vote.

Governance of Good Citizenship means that the citizens must be empowered so that the power of governance flows from them and the communities they belong to (i.e., from their barangays) from ground up, rather than from Malacanang or top down. With this structure, good leadership should follow because governance based on a committed and informed citizenry will inevitably and eventually produce good and leaders.

Is this possible? The answer is that the current Constitution and existing laws, specially the Local Government Code, already provide us with the opportunity to establish a governance of strong and informed citizens. It is a Constitution and system of laws where, if harnessed properly, the power of governance should flow from ground (the Barangay) up to Malacanang, and not the other way around.

But, sad to say, many, if not most, of us are unaware of the powers currently invested in the people by the current Constitution and implementing laws that could and would allow us now to have a government truly of the people, for the people, and by the people.

Let us, citizens all, each study and understand the provisions of the Constitution and its empowering laws, such as the Local Government Code, and claim our nation's true democratic destiny! (REE, 11 July 2019)

....

55
Goodbye?

Is it, as the old song goes,
"Time now to say goodbye?"
Well, only God truly knows
When we will cross the sky.
I know that day will come.
It is the "when" I cannot say.
God chooses for all, not some,
Even as we kneel and pray.

Should I then say goodbye?
Perhaps soon, but not today.
But even as the night might die,
It is only God who can truly say.
So rather than say goodbye,
Please pray today for me
That in God's towering sky
His Face I will shortly see.

Parting does not mean forever.
We are meant to meet again.
We are meant to be together
At that distant Kingdom's end.
Weep not for me for when I go
To beyond that far off bend,
My friendship will stay like so,

I know it will never

(Raf Evangelista, 13 March , 2023)

....

56
Passive Acceptance Will Not Work In Democracy, Which Is Defined As: A Government Of, For, And BY THE PEOPLE

A survey was conducted some years ago on how people, specially at Barangay level, understand the 1987 Constitution and the Local Government Code, specially the empowering provisions of both.

The survey revealed that the Local Government Code's provisions were either poorly understood or ignored by officials, while their constituents knew little or nothing about it, not especially their role in the barangay's governing processes.

In almost ten years of supposed implementation, the Local Government Code's intent to expand the democratic space, empower the community, and activate local or economy found no resonance in the consciousness or acts of those surveyed. The structures and processes it prescribed were largely inoperative. At best, the officials simply simulated them in ways that enabled them to manipulate the community and its resources in order to stay in power.

Many too were unaware that the 1987 Consitution mandates that "Sovereignty resides in the People, and that all governmental authority emanates from them." Far less were aware of the Local Government Code grants to the residents of each Barangay, acting collectively as a Barangay Assembly, the power to be the supreme governing body in the Barangay, in fulfillment of the mandate of the Constitution.

Field verification and analyses of the findings led to the conclusion that neither autonomy nor democracy had advanced to any significance. Quite the contrary, it regressed as money became the driving force of grassroots politics. The introduction of the internal revenue allotment (IRA) for local governments, coupled with the ballooning of congressional pork barrel allowances, fueled the use of patronage as an instrument of political control on all levels. This enabled family dynasties to dominate politics as never before -- on all levels starting with the barangays.

With the rise of money politics, governance of the feudal variety came al ve with a vengeance. Traditional politics produced trapos and trapo governance became the vogue. Contrary to the Code's intent to decentralize power and empower the people, trapo leaders became even more powerful and in firmer control of the grassroots. With patronage and paternalism in full bloom, it was no surprise that elections favored them, turning barangay constituencies into fiefdoms ruled by family dynasties that in turn owed their allegiance to Big Bosses at municipal, provincial and national levels.

Why this happened despite the empowering provisions of the Local Government Code could be ascribed to two reasons. When it became law: a) the trapos, back in office soon after EDSA I, simply ignored its transparency and accountability provisions, and b) no one bothered to inform the people of the Code's provisions – especially of their mandated role in local governance.

For instance, people were not informed that the Code had set huge allocations to their barangay government – for operations and for capitalizing local development. Nor were they informed that they had a say in how these were to be spent. They didn't know that

they now had direct charge of their community's affairs --
as members of the Barangay Assembly, the local
parliament. They didn't know they had the power of
Recall, that they could actually remove or replace
abusive or corrupt officials. Nor were they told of their
right of Initiative and Referendum, whereby they could
directly initiate legislation or nullify undesirable
ordinances.

What was so disappointing about the survey's
revelations was that no one -- not even the interior and
local government department -- bothered to undertake
an information campaign on its new and empowering
provisions. Thus, uninformed, kept in the dark, the
people remained powerless while the trapos who were
already in power feasted on their powerlessness and
became more powerful. Local autonomy remained a
pipe-dream, as did local development despite the billions
flowing to the barangays year after year.

Keeping the people in the dark and uninvolved
served the trapos well. They could carry on as if the
Code had changed nothing of the old system, and stay
in power ad infinitum. It didn't help that the putative
bebeficiaries of the Code, the 42,000 barangays in the
country, did nothing to propagate its provisions and
claim ownership of the democracy promised by the
Constitution and the Code.

Should the Local Government Code be
scrapped? Is the Code an unqualified failure?

The answer to both questions is a resounding
"No!"

EDSA I was not supposed to be the end all and
be all of the Revolution. That was merely the initial step.
Nor was it supposed to culminate with passage of the
1987 Constitution and implementing laws like the Local
Government Code. That was the second step. The third
step was to educate nationwide the people about their
sovereign right to govern the country under the 1987
Constitution and the Local Government Code. The fourth

and final step was for the people to enforce their sovereign right and actively rule and govern their respective Barangays through their Barangay Assemblies. These last and final steps still have to be pursued and implemented for People Power to finally succeed.

Government is everybody's business. You cannot expect good governance if you're not involved!

....

Photos

Pic 1 – Osaka, Japan with Marilou

Pic 2 – Lithuanian Congressional Medal Of honor

Pic3 – Awarding of Lithuanian Congressional Medal of Honor with Lithruanian Ambassador Meilunas

Pic 4 – Osaka, Japan with Marilou

Pic 5 – Flying, Sucic, Zamabales, Philippines

Pic6 – VP Leni Robredo with my grandchildren

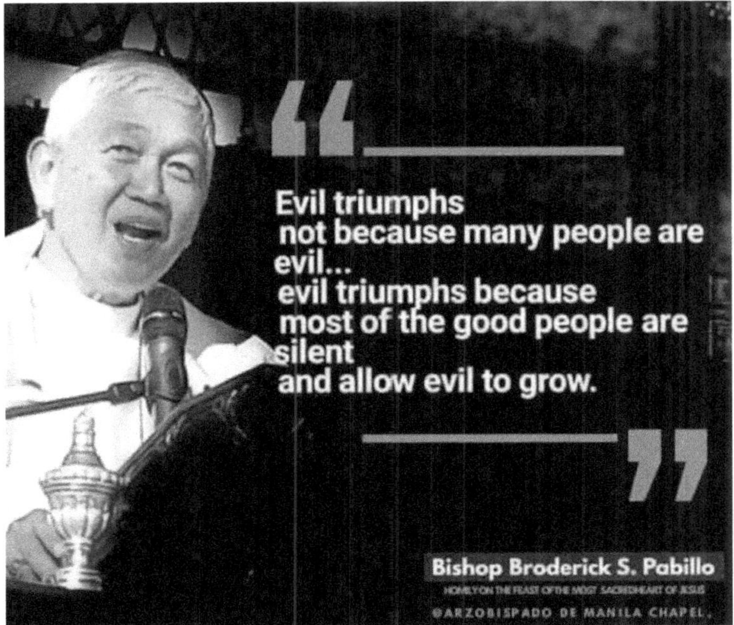

Pic7 – Self-explanatory

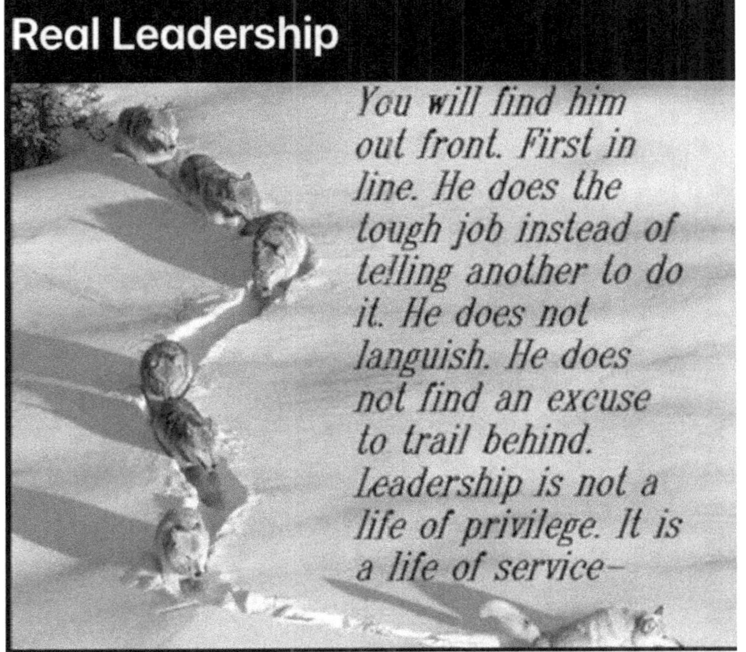

Pic8 – Self-explanatory

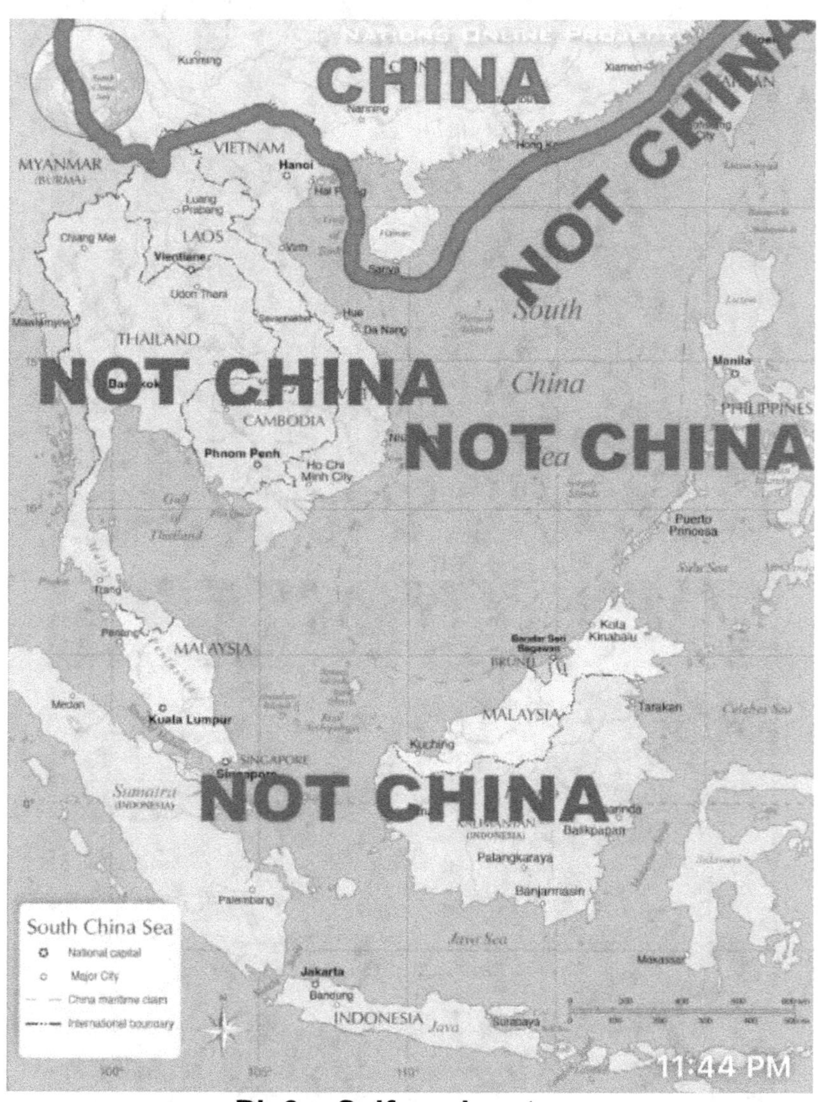

Pic9 – Self-explanatory

Pic10 – Makati Red Cross which I founded

www.ingramcontent.com/pod-product-compliance
Lightning Source LLC
Chambersburg PA
CBHW051754250726